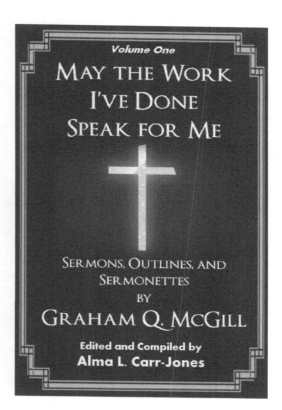

Volume One

MAY THE WORK
I'VE DONE
SPEAK FOR ME

SERMONS, OUTLINES, AND
SERMONETTES
BY

GRAHAM Q. McGILL

Edited and Compiled by
Alma L. Carr-Jones

FOREWORD

May the Work I've Done Speak for Me

While it is an honor to write this foreword about Bro. Graham Q. McGill, there is no way that I can truly speak about the preaching, teaching, love, dedication, and sacrifice that he has shown to several generations of the Church while on various ministerial fields. The title of this piece, from one of his favorite songs, is an apt title for this foreword of a dedicated gospel preacher as he.

In a deviation from the traditional foreword, I have decided to include one of his sermons on the life of the apostle Paul. While going through the plethora of sermons that Bro. McGill has written during the course of his life, the following sermon, Come Before Winter, spoke to my heart, and I am sure that it will to yours as well.

Submitted by
Alma L. Carr–Jones

COME BEFORE WINTER

2 Timothy 4:9–22

Introduction

Writing from a dark prison dungeon, Paul says to Timothy, his son in the faith...v. 9–21.

The last words written by Paul, from what he had said in the preceding verses, "I am now ready..."

Discussion

I. The seriousness of the request is more understandable when we view the circumstances surrounding it.

1. Tired and worn because of his extensive labors (his missionary journeys) beginning with Acts 13.

2. Soon to be martyred – soon to be put to death because he dared to preach the gospel; to say his last goodbye to many brethren he had known and loved (like an hourglass, the sand was running out.)

3. He wanted to see his close friends (no enemies; other friends mentioned at the end of the chapter verses 19–21). Of course Paul had the LORD as a friend, but he had so conducted himself that he had cultivated warm and lasting friendships.

4. Traveling might be difficult after winter set in,

especially sea travel – Paul knew what it was to be in sea storms (in three shipwrecks in the deep, night and day). 2 Corinthians 11:25; Acts 27

5. If not then, then, maybe NEVER – people have a way of putting off things when not done at a certain time.

THINK what it would have been like for Timothy to have gotten there a month or two after Paul was executed!

So, Paul said, "Do thy diligence" (do your best), if at all possible.

II. The LARGER or GREATER message is the application to those of us today, who are faced with similar circumstances, maybe in a longer framework of time. BUT we too, must put off these frail bodies and meet GOD in judgement one day. MANY are unprepared! Jeremiah 8:20 and Matthew 25:13.

1. Our lives may be compared to the SEASONS of the year, spring, summer, fall and winter.

a. Spring – infancy thru adolescence

Time of joy, gaiety, unbounded strength, not a worry in the world (food, clothes, shelter, etc., aches & pains)

b. Then comes summer – young manhood and womanhood in the prime of life. A person reaching maturity able to be of service and produce.

c. Fall – a beautiful time of the year (trees turning) OLD
AGE. It's interesting to see people who have lived
well and wisely in the autumn of their lives. It
makes one stop and think, when spring and summer
have gone, fall and winter are approaching.

d. Just as sure as two follows one, and three follows two,
and four follows three, or as B follows A, and C
follows B, and D follows C, and summer follows
spring and fall follows summer, so winter will
follow Fall – TIME of DYING.

The importance of coming to CHRIST should touch
every soul today because we are approaching the
winter of our lives.

2. Don't let anything stop you!

Fear: can't live perfect lives

Selfishness: Have to give up some things (Anything you
have to give up isn't good for you anyway.)
Anything the LORD gives you is what will help
you.

Don't think it will always be spring and summer time.

III. Old Man (death) who challenged a group of young
men to a race – even though they thought they could

easily outrun him, they dropped out, one by one. The old man got off to a slow start but overtook each one. He and the young man would fall out. The last young man could hear the old man gaining on him and also heard him chanting; I got Adam. I got Methuselah. I got Abraham, and I will get you. The young man looked back and saw a grinning skull – death. Hebrews 9:27; Ecclesiastes 12

Conclusion

Can you bring yourself to believe in CHRIST?

Repent of your sins.

Confess your faith in CHRIST.

And be baptized.

THEN come now, whatever stage of life you are in, **you need JESUS!**

TABLE OF CONTENTS

Come Before Winter iii

About the Author 3

Joshua Takes Command 5

A Personal Talk with Self... 10

Brotherly Love... 15

The Unsearchable Riches of Christ 18

Building on a Good Foundation.................................. 21

Treasure in Earthen Vessels....................................... 31

I Will Teach You the Good and Right Way................... 37

Church Growth Now 39

Church Growth in the Community 48

Do All in the Name of the Lord.................................. 52

Getting Ready for Space Travel.................................. 54

God's Grace: Past, Present, and Future 56

Grace and Its Demands 63

The Culmination of the Treatise on Grace 69

How Long the Night?... 79

Mechanical Instrumental Music 84

The Healing of the Ten Lepers................................... 87

Marriage 91

    Marriage Ceremony Example 1........................... 96

    Marriage Ceremony Example 2........................... 101

Other Sheep I Have.. 104

Famous Lies of the Devil 106

Pressing On.. 110

Pressing On – Sermon.. 113

Some Threes of Sin.. 116

Correcting Mistakes.. 118

The Importance of God's Word 121

People Christ Praised.. 123

Prodigal Son 127

Reaching for the Son in '81 129

Saved by Fear 131

Stop, Look, and Listen.. 133

Teaching and Admonishing One Another 137

What Wait I For?... 139

When God Laughs at a Man 142

Whose Servant are You? 145

Some Women Needed, Some Not, in the Church 148

ABOUT THE AUTHOR

On October 1, 1927, a baby boy was born to the union of Edmund Lewis and Laura Lee Wallace McGill of Duck River, Hickman Co., TN. The baby was later to be known as Graham Quitman McGill.

He grew up on a farm, attending church and elementary school in the Center Star community. He attended O.H. Bernard High School in Centerville, TN and finally to Nashville Christian Institute in Nashville, TN.

By the time he went to NCI, he was already preaching on a limited basis. But at NCI he took some special studies and began preaching on a more regular basis.

His preaching career, having spanned some 79 years, has covered a wide area, beginning with congregations in Middle Tennessee: his home church; Ft. Cooper, Primm Springs, TN; Arrow Rock, Williamsport, TN; Gaines St., Lawrenceburg, TN; Columbia Ave., Centerville, TN; Dry Fork, Hampshire, TN; Pleasant Union, Hampshire TN; Burns Spring, Columbia, TN; Broadway St., Mt. Pleasant, TN; Allison Ave., Hohenwald, TN; Linden, TN. His labors later spread to Martin, TN; Union City, TN; Kenton, TN; Paducah, Ky, Brookport, Il; and St. Louis, MO. Through his efforts, the church in Kenton had its beginning. He also established the church in Kellar, VA and helped in establishing congregations at Hohenwald, Linden, and Booker Ridge, Hampshire. More than half of his preaching career has been spent at Vine St. Church of Christ in Union City, Tennessee, where he has been since 1971.

His work has carried him into 25 States and numerous cities. He has appeared on National and Local Lectureships and has been involved in Radio and TV broadcasting. Hundreds obeyed the gospel through his teaching.

Wherever he has lived he has been involved in civic and community affairs.

JOSHUA TAKES COMMAND

Joshua 1

1. Wherever he walked – from wilderness of Zion to the Euphrates River unto the great season (the west coast)

2. No man would be able to prevail against him, for GOD would always be there. (Never fail nor forsake.)

3. Joshua was to be strong and courageous; observe to "do as he was commanded; not turning to the right or to the left."

4. Book of law not to depart, will make you prosperous and successful

5. First command given was Prepare!

6. Tribes on the east were to travel with their brethren fighting with them until they were settled in their land. Then they could return and enjoy their possessions. (Failure of one is failure of all and vice versa.)

7. They promised to do whatsoever they were commanded to do, as they had promised Moses. "Those who rebel shall be put top death." Cut off.

Chapter 2

1. Two spies sent out

danger and escape; knowledge of GOD of Israel; request of Rahab and conditions of fulfillment; report of spies very different from those of the first mission given in Deuteronomy 27.

Chapter 3–6

Crossing the Jordan; memorial stones; Commander of the LORD's army; conquest of Jericho.

Chapter 7

Sin in the Camp (Achan's sin), there was a defeat at Ai and as a result, the people lost heart. Joshua 7:8–11

Crossing the Jordan

Chapter 8 (and Deuteronomy 27)

Victory given over Ai – subsequent reading of the law before the entire congregation, (women and children included) Israel was divided to bless and to curse, verse 30–35.

Chapter 9

1. Fear of Israel caused Gibeonites to use deception to

have Israel form an alliance with them.

2. As a result, the Gibeonites were made woodcutters and water carriers for Israel.

Chapter 10

1. When the LORD fights for you – verse 11, "Hailstones rained down and more died from the hailstones than from the swords of Israel because the LORD fought for Israel." In verses 13 and 14 we read these words, "And the sun stood still and the moon stopped until the nation took vengeance upon its enemies. Isn't this written in the Book of Joshua? So the sun stopped in the middle of the sky and delayed its setting almost a full day. 14 There has been no day like it before nor since, when the LORD listened to a man, because the LORD fought for Israel."

Chapters 11–22

1. "So Joshua took the entire land, in keeping with all that the LORD had told Moses. Joshua then gave it as an inheritance to Israel according to their tribal allotments. After this, the land had rest from war." (Joshua 11:23) (CSB)

Chapter 23

Joshua Bids Israel Farewell.

1 "A long time after the LORD had given Israel rest
from all the enemies around them, Joshua was old,
advanced in age." (CSB)

2 "So Joshua summoned all Israel, including its elders,
leaders, judges, and officers, and said to them, 'I am
old, advanced in age,' (CSB)

3 "and you have seen for yourselves everything the
LORD your God did to all these nations on your
account, because it was the LORD your God who
was fighting for you." (CSB)

8 "Instead, be loyal to the LORD your God, as you have
been to this day." (CSB)

14 "I am now going the way of the whole earth, and you
know with all your heart and all your soul that none
of the good promises the LORD your God made to
you has failed. Everything was fulfilled for you; not
one promise has failed." (CSB)

Conclusion

Israel was victorious over the land that the LORD had

promised them because they kept their eyes on the
LORD GOD and obeyed His commands. And as
Joshua instructed Israel and as we have been
instructed down through the Bible, though leaders
come and go, if we keep our hands in GOD's hands,
we will be victorious in the work of the Church, for
GOD fights for us.

A PERSONAL TALK WITH SELF

Maybe we all do this at times, at least we ought to have a talk with ourselves ever so often, especially when caught between two opinions, trying to make a decision.

Words of others have a tremendous influence on our lives. Depending on what is said, life can be made better or worse. Untold harm may come from ONE wrong word, while endless good can come from one good word. We can make or destroy someone by our words. Solomon said, "A word firstly spoken is like apples of gold in pitchers of silver." Proverbs 25:11

Back to the personal talk to self: what we say to ourselves is of vast importance. Since we don't have to impress anybody, we can be honest with ourselves. And what we habitually say to ourselves, tells us what kind of people we are.

Let's look at three people in the Bible who talked to themselves and see what it reveals about them. Also, consider any lessons that might be helpful to us. The persons to be discussed are:

I. The Woman with the Issue of Blood – Matthew, Mark, and Luke

II. The Successful Farmer – Luke 12:16–19

III. The Prodigal Son – Luke 15

<u>The Woman with the Issue of Blood</u> (Matthew 9:20–22; Mark 5:25–34; Luke 8:43:48) – Reading from Matthew's account, we begin with verse 20. Viewing her life, she might have said some very distressing things and have told the truth. Her life had been hard: for 12 years she had suffered a continued flow of blood from her body (a disease that made her morally unclean). That robbed her of wifehood and motherhood; probably the only positive thing in her life was that she was a woman of considerable, independent means.

She, determined to find a cure, went from doctor to doctor and finally spent all she had. She finds herself a little more faded, a little weaker, a little closer to the cemetery. She might have lashed out at life, even against GOD, but rather, she says, "I am sick, but I'm not dead; money is gone, but I hear there is a man in the area – named JESUS who has done some unbelievable things. I'm going to see what he can do for me. If I win, I win and if I fail, I won't be any worse off. At least I will have done what I could. If I can just touch his garment, I shall be whole." Her message was a message of **hope**.

It's good to have hope – lose hope and we stop trying:
Getting up when we've been knocked down;
Can't get well; getting a job, etc.

Her conversation to herself set her on a course that paid
off. She met with difficulty on her journey (crowd),
but she kept repeating the message of faith, holding
on to hope. And finally, she got close enough to
touch the hem of His garment and was made whole.
(In my mind's eye, I can imagine her having to
perhaps crawl on her knees because of the press of
the crowd. She had to be on her knees because she
was just stretching to touch the hem of his garment,
not the shoulder, arm, leg, etc. in my mind's eye,
she on her knees where life had knocked her to, but
even from that position…)
What are we saying to ourselves in times of difficulty?
Get close to JESUS and keep moving. Remember
Paul's statement in Philippians 4:13, "I can do all
things through CHRIST which strengtheneth me."
KJV

The Successful Farmer (Luke 12:16–19) – The Rich Fool or The Successful Farmer is a second person who had a conversation with self. He was honorable, successful and upright as people looked at him. But we see a different person, perhaps the real man, as we listen to him in conversation with himself. We see a selfish man totally wrapped up in himself. It's "I" and "my," even talks as if he was in charge of his life and time. GOD classifies him as a fool. (v. 20) GOD's message to future generations, v. 21.

Person Number Three – The one usually referred to as the prodigal son is found in Luke 15. If you begin reading with verse 11 you will find that his conversation with himself begins in verse 17 and goes through 19. When he came to himself … he was not acting like himself as he really was – a gracious father's son. He had not been looking at himself; not studying himself; not thinking of his real condition and his real want.

Once he comes to himself, he begins to talk to himself, as if to say, "What am I doing out here? I can do better!" By his words, you can tell that he was thinking of home (verses 17, 18, 19). He compares

back home, (where he left from) to (a far country)
where he is now and forms a conclusion. I will
arise...etc.; I will confess all – make a clean breast
of all. I will throw myself upon my father's mercy.
(verse 19)

After the talk with himself, he acted on his decision.

(verse 20) "He arose..."

He was received gladly and joyfully.

The Lesson to Us:

If we, after serving in GOD's house, decide to leave
and try a different way of life – know it leads to
no good end. GOD will let us go and He will take
us back if we repent and confess our wrongs.

Let's all have a talk with ourselves and see how we
stand.

BROTHERLY LOVE

Psalm133:1; 1 Peter 1:22; Hebrews 13:1

Introduction

1. We heard something said last week about Brotherhood Week. As I understood it, special efforts were being put forth to bring about better relations between the human race. All mankind should be united as brothers, seeing we have a common CREATOR. (Made of one blood) Acts 16:26

In Genesis 13 Abraham said, "I pray that there be no strife between me and thee, because we are brethren." (All descended from Adam and Eve.) (KJV)

2. Especially fitting for GOD's people to live as brethren because we have the same redeemer, CHRIST: the same Master, Matthew 23:8

Members of the same family, cherish the same hope, eat at the same table, subjected to the same trials and temptations and sorrows.

3. CHRIST died that all might be brethren, Ephesians 2:14; Galatians 3:26–28

4. Hatred and division may be expected in the world, but not on the inside of the Church. It is childish.

I trust the day will speedily come when the church of our LORD will no longer be referred to as the White church and Colored (Black) church. What is Brotherly Love?

Discussion

I. GOD's Universal Currency

    1. Will work anywhere

        a. In the jungles of Africa

        b. To those who dislike you for no reason. Show them that you love them.

    2. Some love, visit, and trade with their own kind

II. Divine Heat of the Universe

    1. Try planting corn in good soil in January. While it is bitter cold and freezing.

    2. Wait until springtime, sun changes its course, rays penetrate this old earth and thaws it out; birds come back from the south; vegetation springs up and all nature takes on a form of life.

    3. Where the Church of my LORD is torn asunder by malice, strife, discord, and brethren are at war one with the other, there is no need to plant the seed of the kingdom.

III. The Badge of Christianity

    1. "All men shall know."

IV. The Fulfilling if the Law

    Romans 13:8–10

V. Greatest Thing in the World 1 Corinthians 13

    1. Many sit in the pews, listen to the sermon, take the LORD's supper and yet, won't speak to their brother.

Conclusion

    1. You can't skip your fellowman and go to GOD 1 John 4:20 if you have hatred in your heart for any man, your worship here is hindered and Heaven will never be your home.

    2. Let us become educated in the primitive principles of Christianity and learn to love one another as GOD and CHRIST loved(s) us.

THE UNSEARCHABLE RICHES OF CHRIST

Topic: Speaking the Truth in Love

Introduction

Much is said about **riches** in the book of Ephesians. Rich in mercy, riches of grace and in chapter 3 and verse 8, Paul speaks of the exalted privilege of preaching to the Gentiles. Certainly, Paul has reference to the gospel and what it holds for those who accept it. 1 Corinthians 2:7–9 "Unsearchable," in that the blessings are many and beyond the comprehension of the natural man. Herein is found love, pardon, comfort, wisdom, happiness, and a life of eternal bliss at the end.

Speaking the Truth in Love:

The riches we enjoy in CHRIST, should be shared with others. But the success in doing so depends on the way it is done. The <u>manner</u> of saying a thing is of as much importance as the <u>thing</u> said. Note Proverbs 25:11. Apples of Gold in Silver Pitchers are fine, but when/if we take the apples out and start throwing them at each other's heads, they become instruments of danger, of great pain, of much harm and even murder.

Words fitly spoken are fine – can do much good, though

they may be good and true, if they are uttered in a rude insolent, arrogant and offensive manner, they will probably result in evil rather than good.

The question of manner is worth taking into consideration by those whose responsibility it is to instruct, advise, rebuke, and exhort his fellowman. It was said of the shepherd of King Admetus, whose

"Words were simple words enough,
And yet he used them so
That what in other mouths was rough
In his, seemed musical and low."

Many good Christians are unsympathetic, can't enter into the feelings of others … so what they intend for good leaves the person on the other side irritated and wounded. Then there are some who have so much wisdom, sympathy, and tact, that even in doing a severe thing – even in finding serious fault or refusing to grant some request – they were able to make a friend for life. The difference is in the how it is done. (Golden Rule) Note 1 Peter 3:15.

You know how prone we are to speak the truth without regards to the feelings of others and when people become defensive, we satisfy ourselves by saying, "I told them the truth." Well, speaking the truth should never become a means of exalting self, but to change lives.

Two men sowing seed: The one while a rough wind is blowing or when surround by birds which devour it as it falls – the other when the atmosphere is calm and no creatures are near to prevent it from falling into the ground.

If a preacher in preaching the gospel assumes a severe, harsh overbearing manner, then, though what he speaks be GOD's truth, his chance of really doing good to those who hear him is greatly diminished. Show people that you love them, then you can tell them the truth that condemns them and yet awaken no bitterness; you may show them how wrong they are and only make them thankful to you for setting them right.

To accomplish this, become a follower of Jesus Christ, the greatest preacher Who ever graced this earth. He was the very embodiment of truth and always exhibited love.

BUILDING ON A GOOD FOUNDATION

In all our lives there have been pivotal and/or soul–
touching moments that will live on as long as our brains give
us recall. These are a few of such reflection times for me.

Reflections from November 12, 1995 – I've just returned
from what I consider to be one of the greatest, most fulfilling
experiences of my life – the 75th Anniversary of the Midwest
Church of CHRIST in Louisville, KY. Many people figure in
these 75 years of planting and maintaining this church
throughout the years. This was done under the leadership of
Bro. G. P. Bowser, Marion Holt, Earl Dulan, and Frank
McGill, along with a staunch membership of both men and
women. Some of those who were there in the 1920s still have
offspring in the congregation. A foundation of FAITH was
built by each congregation for the oncoming generation. This
brings to mind the biblical examples of Lois, Eunice and
Timothy.

Vine St. has been around some 75 or 80 (*100+ years to
date*). It is still here because somebody held the ropes and
shouldered the load and if it continues, somebody will have
to keep holding ropes and shouldering loads. The theme for
the week was "A Diamond Shining in a World of Darkness."

CHRIST came to earth somewhere BC 4 or 2. He came to show man how to live and to offer him a better way of life. While here on earth He said, "As long as I am in the world, I am the LIGHT of the world." Being now at home with His FATHER, He has the church (His spiritual body) as the light of the world.

We think the world is rough (and it is) but think what it would be like if the church didn't exist. The best people in the world are in the church of CHRIST. There may be some bad people in the church, but the worst people in the world aren't in the church, despite the bad element of the church. The church is right; that I'm sure of.

For the church to serve its purpose in this cruel, wicked world, we must shine as lights (sun, moon, and stars) in the world. Matthew5:16 Be more than a carnal individual; take on the divine nature and show the world a better way of life. When you are misused, misjudged, and misunderstood – when people ridicule, laugh or speak lightly of you, remember that you are *holding rope and shouldering loads* for the next generation, so keep stepping.

Reflections from November 6, 1995 – Today's activities are focusing in on those who have been members of the church 30 years or more. The theme is Salute to the Steadfast. The word steadfast suggests being fixed, settled, having taken a seat as not to be moved. These are the kind of people who will or can keep the church alive in a place for 75 years. And those who are thus steadfast will not go unrewarded if they continue in the faith. In the Scripture, the reward is often spoken of in terms of a crown, a crown of life, an incorruptible crown, a crown that <u>fadeth</u> not away.

Crown, a noun, referring to a wreath or band for the head – worn as a mark of victory or honor. People often make mention of receiving a golden crown and we sing the song, "The Golden Crown," however, the Bible doesn't say it's gold. *(Revelation 14:14 speaks of JESUS having a crown of gold on His head.)* Let us then take a look at a few passages of Scripture that talk about the crown as the final reward of the faithful/steadfast. While gold is one of the most precious metals of the earth, the term also bespeaks permanence. The Bible speaks of the victory of faithful Christians in terms of a crown in: 1 Corinthians 9:25; 2 Timothy 2:5; 2 Timothy 4:8; James 1:12; 1 Peter 5:4; Revelation 2:10 and maybe Revelations 3:11. From the passages of Scripture listed above we learn:

1. Just as athletes, discipline themselves and run races to win prizes, even so, Christians run a spiritual race to win a prize. (The first was corruptible, the second incorruptible or not subject to decay and destruction.)

24

2. Paul further expressed the assurance that after having fought a good fight, etc. he would receive a crown of righteousness "at that day." He also expressed the confidence that all who love the LORD's appearing would receive a crown.

3. The man that endureth temptation shall at the time of trial receive a crown of life, as promised by the LORD – promised to those who love him.

4. Faithful "elders" will receive a crown of glory – that fades not away.

5. Despite the things a Christian may suffer, there is the promise of better things to come. Be faithful unto death and receive a crown of life.

6. Satan or his agents may take our crown through fear and discouragement.

7. In reiterating, none of the passages say the crown is gold; however, the promise of a crown should inspire hope when we can't see the need of going on. To know that there is another life beyond this one – free from...

We are in the land of the dying journeying toward the land of the living. Whether saved or unsaved, we're headed toward an endless life in Heaven or in Hell.

Further Reflections from November 6, 1995 – As referenced in Matthew 25:14–21, every child of GOD looks for the LORD's return. It will be a time of vindication and avengement. We don't know when the LORD will return, but we shouldn't just sit and twiddle our thumbs – we must be busy with our responsibilities, in other words not just wait but work, etc.

Such things as:

I. Be responsible for the development of your spiritual life. Invest in study, learn what you need to listen to and watch on TV.

II. Be mindful of your responsibility of keeping the church alive. Somebody kept it alive and sacrificed as servants of old to sit under tents, etc. be mindful of your attendance and be ready in every good work.

III. Preserve the faith by standing on and preaching (teaching) the Word.

Those entrusted with the talents were responsible 'til the master returned. We need to remember that. Folk get tired too quickly and need more than "a little dab" of good works to stay encouraged.

IV. Be mindful of your financial responsibility. GOD has given to us to see what we will do with it.

Reflections from November 7, 1995 – Continuing with

the thought from yesterday, this session is designed to reach and further stimulate/encourage those of the young adult age level to build a foundation of faith and commitment in the interest of the generations to come. No doubt, you are reading this book today because someone before you laid the same kind of foundation within themselves to ground and stabilize you in the faith. Be reminded of the bridge builder who built a bridge <u>after</u> he crossed over the river – for the youth following him. Also there is the traveler who pumped water to leave at the well so the next traveler could prime the pump (the next traveler, he probably would never see).

It is important that those coming after you, see in you a life based on faith and commitment, especially now because of the kind of world we live in – a cruel, wicked, fun–crazy and materialistic one. CHRIST needs to be lifted up before the "now" and coming generation and made to see that the way of CHRIST is the only sure and successful way of life. They need to see your continued faith even if Satan knocks you down and tries to take whatever you have. They need to see and hear you say, "Try JESUS He will make everything alright!"

They need to see and hear that your foundation is one that stands in the faith of facts as opposed to the faith of conscience. Both are important. A foundation that has the word of GOD as its source. Matthew 7:22–27 – Picture a man building a house of life/characters. 2 Corinthians 4:13; 5:7. **Faith in GOD, His Word, His promises, maybe even His threats, allows us to trust Him!** The fact that you know He does many miraculous things without miracles brings relief under the most trying and hopeless circumstances and this faith should be evident for all to see. (In your quest for things, remember the best way to get them is to let GOD be first in your life. Matthew 6:31.)

Commit yourself to the point that you know what you believe and be determined that nothing will turn you around. Exodus. Going out on a high diving board, and then when you see the long jump between there and the pool – don't turn around … Jump anyhow!

You might be saying, "I can't do that!" Well, listen to this: Moses, Gideon, and Jonah thought this at first, too, but they became committed individuals. So, make the decision to be committed in your life and take it one day at a time. You must be committed by continuing to submit yourself to GOD no matter the trials.

There are two kinds of submission – forced and voluntary. We shouldn't want GOD to force us to submit but voluntarily do so because of Who He is and what He is doing for us.

I. Submit our will.

II. Submit to Him Our Talents and Abilities

1. The ones we use for our livelihood
III. Submit Our Time
IV. Submit Our Possessions
   Remember the story of the rich young ruler in
   Matthew 19:16–22 and the widows mite in Luke
   21:1–4.
V. Submit to Him Our Cares

That the Generations to Come might Know – Let
Matthew Zion (the church) rejoice. There is not enough joy
in the church. If you're happy, inform your face.

Mark the bulwarks
1. GOD – He is alive and on the throne.
2. Bible Greatest Book – Teach them to study it.
3. Church – Let them see your love and respect for it.

Reflections of November 9, 1995 – We are going to focus
our attention on church growth and development,
encouraging all members of the church to become part of the
process.

The LORD is concerned about the growth of His church
as seen in many of the parables He set forth, especially the
Mustard Seed Parable and The Leaven. When we take a
careful and serious look into church growth, we see a need
for human/personal involvement. Even prayer alone won't

get the job done.

The church was planned and set in motion with only 12 men. They preached and one the first day, we find people obeying the gospel and people being added to the church. (about 3,000) It continued to grow in Jerusalem and finally when, because of persecution, the church was scattered abroad. Those who were scattered went everywhere preaching the word. (Everybody was involved.) This happened under adverse circumstances/conditions – threats, beatings, etc. et Cox Within some thirty years, the gospel was preached to the whole known world. Colossians 1:23 They knew the Word. What about you? (Some of you know *everything else.*)

We have a responsibility toward growing the church in this age and century in which we live. Everybody wants the church to grow, **but** they say, "Ya'll do it; don't count on me." We all have a responsibility toward the lost. On our part, there should be an attitude of compassion, concern, selflessness, gentleness and assistance. The responsibility may be both congregate and individual – special one on one contact. (Mention the crusades.)

Mark 16:15, a passage that used to scare me to death, may be reduced to *one on one*. Each one can reach the ones of "our" world – next door, across the street, next street over, etc. The church or the Christian needs to make their presence felt in the community in which they exist. Let the unsaved see what salvation through Christ <u>has done</u> for you. Prove yourself a good neighbor. Then share with them the good news of the gospel (at least what you know). [I don't know enough.] 1 Peter 3:15 and Matthew 5:16. Sometimes we may need to go out of our way. (*JESUS and Samaria, John 4.*)

Remember, nobody is too bad or awful to be saved: or that we can't share with them the love of GOD. Also, remember, there may be some people that only you can reach. Maybe some special one watched you, so in turn, reach out to be the love. You are urged to put forth a definite effort on a definite person for a definite time.

To the unsaved, you need to become a part: to enroll in the greatest business in the world – soul saving. Shine as the stars and gain a home in Heaven (FRCB) and be faithful – don't worry about success. And don't forget Andrew, who brought with him Simon Peter, his brother. (John 1:40–41). Little is said of Andrew in the Bible, but his brother, Peter, went on to become a star. Everybody knew who Peter was, but who brought him to JESUS? Just remember, you don't have to be a star to be in GOD's show.

TREASURE IN EARTHEN VESSELS

Thank you for the opportunity to address you at this time – a time to honor those who have given themselves to and for the preaching of the gospel – men who felt the power of GOD's penetrating presence. They are willing, just as the first century preachers were, to spend and be spent for the cause of GOD. It is befitting that you have dedicated this lectureship to the memory of the great preachers who walked before us. Through their sacrifices, the church in many places is alive today. Some walked miles to their appointments; others received little compensation for their labors. We need to remember this when we must be guaranteed a "certain" amount of money to go and preach the gospel.

Bro. Penn contacted me some months ago to ask if I would fill a spot at the Annual Lectureship Banquet, that spot finally being the keynote speaker. It was left to me to decide what I would talk about. And when I had finished that lesson, Bro. Penn called to assign me a subject, so I started on another lesson. I will give you a little bit of both – the first one entitled, "The Future of the Church – Staying the Course."

The future of the church should be a matter of concern to every Christian, everyone. There is no guarantee that the church in any given location will continue to be the church as presented in the Bible or as we know it today. Some have already ceased to be, and some are asking the question, "Is this the 1st century church, or should we look for another?" Of course, there will always be a people of GOD somewhere. However, to ensure the survival of the church in any given locality, we must stay the course.

STAY, meaning to remain/continue in; stand firm. COURSE meaning, a path leading from one point to another, an accustomed procedure. Thus, we must stay in, remain in, continue in the path where we want to go and doing so by the prescribed procedure or process. In Acts 2:42, the Jerusalem Church once established, stayed the course by following the apostles' doctrine and so must we. And when we wonder who speaks for the COC today, just know it is still the apostles who speak. Their record (not on tape) is our guide, not Dr. So and So, nor Reverend So and So, not even Bro. So and So.

The early church had problems and they were often resolved by a letter or a visit by an apostle. Let's be reminded of the plea or encouragement of Jude in v. 3 of the book bearing his name. Seeing the danger facing the early church because of false teachers who were invading the church, he exhorts them to earnestly contend, etc. "Once for all times" *that only faith*, which by Jesus Christ through the apostles had been handed down. There was to be no "new revelations." Watch those fellows who have just received a message from the Holy Spirit.

Second Thought

Based on 2 Corinthians 4:7, "We Have This Treasure in Earthen Vessels."

The context centers around the gospel and preachers – The gospel being referred to as a treasure and preachers compared to vessels (earthen vessels). Both are important to the salvation of the souls of men.

A treasure is something of great value because of its cost or of its attachment to someone or some other thing, or its usefulness. A vessel is a hollow or concave utensil designed to holds something and carry it from one place to another. (As a ship, barrel, bottle, bowl, cup, etc.: a person held to be the recipient of a quality).

The gospel is a treasure because of its connection with CHRIST – The Promised One – The Son of GOD – The SAVIOR of the World. The gospel of CHRIST is the means of man's salvation from sin, with its guilty and penalty hence saved from an eternity in hell. (Romans 1:16; 1 Corinthians 15:1–4) This treasure has been placed in earthen vessels – vessels of least value, when compared to vessels of gold, silver, fine brass, etc. or compared to heavenly vessels such as angels, etc.

Man is like his first parent, Adam, of the earth, thus earthy/earthen (a big lump of dirt wrapped in a fine suit and dressed up with a tie around his neck). It is into the hand of such, GOD has put the treasure (the gospel) to be carried to all the world. When the gospel was ready to be carried to the whole world, Jesus Christ commissioned men to carry it. (The Great Commission)

At a later point in time, Paul, as a chosen vessel was commissioned to carry the gospel to the Gentiles. Thus, our text/context where he discusses his manner of handling the treasure and emphasizes the fact that the treasure is in earthen vessels.

The reason for this arrangement is that the excellency of the power (power to save) may be of GOD and not of man. The weaker the vessel, the stronger the power of GOD may appear, thus more value placed on the treasure. Any good that is done, any betterment or transformation of life must be seen as coming from GOD, when we consider the weakness of the messenger.

Many aren't changed because more attention is paid to the messenger than the message. We must be careful messengers, lest we get between the sinner and the gospel.

In salvation from past sin, in this present age, GOD, CHRIST, nor the HOLY SPIRIT will tell one directly what to do.

Note the cases of conversion, especially Cornelius: Feared GOD and prayed to Him always. An angel of GOD came to him and said, "Send men to Joppa and call for Simon, whose surname is Peter; Who shall tell thee words, whereby thou and all thy house shall be saved." (Acts 11:13–14)

Simon Peter gave the message of salvation. (Acts 10:34–43) They believed and were baptized. GOD could have forgiven Cornelius on the spot or told him what to do, but He wouldn't because the treasure was in earthen vessels.

Saul, on a mission to persecute the church in Damascus, met JESUS on the road. Bright light shone round about him; he fell to the earth and heard a voice that said, "Saul, Saul, why persecuteth thou Me?" (Conversation between JESUS and Saul) "What wilt Thou have me to do?" (*Ans.*) "Go into the city, etc."

A certain disciple named Ananias was chosen by GOD as His messenger/vessel. Saul was told to arise and be baptized. Upon doing so, he became a vessel to carry the treasure to others (or acquaint others with the treasure). JESUS, being asked point blank, "What will Thou have me to do?" Could have told him, but He didn't for the treasure is in earthen vessels.

The Ethiopian Eunuch – Philip, as a vessel, had carried

the gospel to Samaria, where upon hearing his preaching, about the kingdom of GOD and the name of JESUS CHRIST, many believed and were baptized. While in the midst of this, the ANGEL spoke to him with news to carry the treasure to a lone man of Ethiopia, a eunuch of great authority, in charge of all of the Queen's treasure. The SPIRIT said to Philip, "Go near, and join thyself to this chariot." He did and conversation between Philip and the Eunuch ensued. (Acts 8:30–34) JESUS is presented to the Eunuch from which he understood the need for baptism and requested the same. Receiving salvation through obedience to the gospel, he went on his way rejoicing.

Of the Angel and the Spirit, neither one made contact with the Eunuch, but with the preacher, the earthen vessel. So, it is ever done! That's why those who went before us gave their all in preaching the gospel. **NOW, let those of us who are entrusted with the proclamation of GOD's word, labor under the charge Paul gave Timothy.** (2 Tim. 4:1–2)

I WILL TEACH YOU
THE GOOD AND RIGHT WAY

1 Samuel 12

Not for Samuel only, this should be the sentiment of every proclaimed preacher and teacher. Four essential duties set down in theses verses – PRAY, TEACH, FEAR and SERVE. The first two are for the preacher or teacher and the last two are for the hearer.

History tells of many men of GOD who followed the intent of Samuel, with many signing their testimony in blood. (Acts 6:4) "We will give ourselves to prayer and to the ministry of the word."

There is only one Good and Right Way and it is not decided in church conventions nor is it determined by each preacher to suit his personal feelings. This was determined by GOD, the FATHER a long time ago, and was executed and ratified by GOD the Son at Calvary and was revealed by GOD the Holy Spirit to men who wrote it that the world might know and understand. (Ephesians 1:3–6; 3:2–7) Preacher must preach what is written!

DUTIES of the Hearers

Fear and Serve – Fear comes first, if we fear, the rest follows.

Fear – Verb

1. To be apprehensive or afraid of; to be fearful or afraid of, as to fear an enemy.

Noun – an emotion excited by threatening evil or impending pain, accompanied by a desire to avoid or escape; apprehension, dread.

2. To look upon with awe or reverence; venerate: as to fear GOD.

Reverence for constituted authority, especially when accompanied by obedience thereto, as the fear of GOD.

Reverence – Verb

To regard with reverence – venerate

To look upon or regard with honor and deference: revere.

CHURCH GROWTH NOW

A Series of Four Parts

Part One

This is a topic of interest to every devoted saint of GOD. It has been a topic of discussion through the decades, even to its position on the scale of growth. In the upper 1900's it was the fastest growing church of that time. At some point it lost its position and has dropped several points on the list. But whether it is at the top, in the middle or at the very bottom, we always want to see the Church grow – right now! (This present time.)

Growth doesn't always have to do with numbers, but souls that are truly converted.

Growth is not in the amount of money we have, but how we use what we have. It is not in the magnificent buildings, but in the quality of the people meeting in the buildings, (the house within the house) not in the multiplicity of activities, but that we carry the missions of the Church as GOD has commanded.

All the aforementioned adds up to the spiritual rather than the physical growth.

How is this accomplished?

By preaching of the word

The parables of Mark 4:26–29; 30–32

The 1st presents the means and manner of growth; the 2nd deals with the extent of its growth. Both begin with the planting/sowing of the seed. Spiritually, the seed is the Word of GOD. (Luke 8:11)

Taking a closer look at the parables recorded in Mark 4:

Verse 26 Man sowing the seed – preacher preaching the word.

No seed sown – nothing grown (no fruitful results)

Verse 27 sower can't do anymore, must wait for nature to take its course, calls for patience and trust . Jas, 5:7

Don't know what effect the preached word may have, but must be preached; wait to see. "GOD gives the increase."

At the proper time, the seed comes up and grows and the sower knows not how.

Verse 28 – gradual growth – 1st the blade (shoot/plant); then the ear; then the full corn in the ear.

Maybe we can expect too much too soon. Some seeds are quicker than others, but in all there is growth.

Verse 29 – until the time of the harvest, there is time/room for growth.

The Second Parable

Verse 30–32

Verse 31 – a grain of mustard seed – less/least/smallest

of all seeds.

Despite its smallness, there is the possibility of bringing forth life, but it must be sown.

Verse 32–here is the extent of its growth as presented– become greater than all herbs (Matthew says it becomes a tree) grew to 8 – 10 feet tall, with the stalk one inch in diameter.

The branches/limbs are great, strong enough that birds of the air could come and rest, with no worry about the branch breaking as they perched thereon.

The church needs to grow to this point.

Conclusion

The principles found in these parables may apply to each member on the church as well as the church in general. So in order for the church to grow, we must grow in the principles of Christianity as found in God's word. The word must be preached and heeded! One must know the Bible; Believe what it teaches; teach what it teaches and do what it teaches.

When the time is right, Christ is coming back for his church at whatever state it is in a given place or as a whole. He will take the faithful home to be with Him forever. You and I must be a part of the church, doing our very best to make the church what the Lord is looking for.

Part Two

Today I am going to continue my discussion on "Church Growth Now." There are only a few, if any, who aren't interested in church growth, even though, some by actions may say, "So long as it doesn't involve me."

The Lord is concerned about the growth of the church as seen in the many parables he used, for example that of the mustard seed and the leaves. Matthew 13:31–35.

In a previous lesson I talked about various ideas about church growth, especially as to what it is not:

–Number only, may have quantity but what about quality

–Large bank account–rather how is it used

–Fine building–but the house within the house

–Multiple activities within

Church growth should be centered around carrying out the mission of God as he has commanded; this is the process of spiritual rather than physical growth. Previously I put great emphasis on the preaching/proclamation of GOD's word, which is the seed of the kingdom. (Mark 4:26–32) Beginning with the preachers, we must preach the same word preached by the apostles and early evangelists in order to be saved and developed into strong effective workers in the church. This means delivering not politically correct, ear-tickling sermons, personal problems/imagined mistreatment, etc. The sermon should not be a time for joking, clowning etc. Leave that to the professional clowns, comedians, politicians, etc. Let's do our job well by faithfully proclaiming the word of GOD.

The strengthening of the church does not stop with the preacher, but every Christian has a part play. One may not be able to do what someone else is doing, but you can use what abilities you have. Some can teach, classroom teaching or one of private settings. 2 Tim. 2:1–2 also 1 Peter 3:15

So maybe you can encourage others – boost someone spirit and keep them going. May exhibit a spirit of friendliness, helpfulness.

Extend an invitation to a service not just at big meeting times.

One thing everybody can do is strive to live a good Christian life– Let people see Jesus in you– At home, on the job, at school, Sports gatherings, on the streets, etc.

Let's grow spiritually so we can grow numerically.

Conclusion

Are you doing all you can the best that you can? Keep on keeping on! Don't let this catch you with your work undone.

Are you here, having not obeyed the gospel to the saving of your soul? JESUS, Who made this possible through his death, burial, and resurrection, now invites you to accept His salvation by simply believing in the love story of Calvary, repenting of every known sin and submitting your body to baptism and you will become a new creature.. Romans 6:1–4, 16–17

NOW IS THE TIME!

Part Three

Church Growth Now

Luke 14: 25 through 33

This is the third in a series of lessons on the church growth – a matter that is close to every faithful Christian heart that is full of the faith. What hinders the growth of the church is that we are not full of what we are trying to push on others. We convert one or two and once they catch a glimpse of our real interest, they leave and join the fastest growing group in the world, the BACKSLIDERS.

If we are to promote church growth, we must be faithful.

WE ARE NOT FAITHFUL:

    1. Until we have a working knowledge of the Bible, especially the New Testament – life of CHRIST, his church, GOD's plan of salvation, how to remain a Christian, the rewards of the righteous and punishment of the wicked.

    2. Until we want to tell others and invite them to

share with us.

3. Until CHRIST and His kingdom mean more to us than anybody or anything in the world.

4. Until we put forth as much effort, if not more, in our religion, as we do in material interests – homes, jobs, sports, recreation, etc.

5. As long as we are irregular in our attendance (absent with our justifiable reasons – be nice to call) No organization (except backsliders) can exist without its meetings, so show interest by attending.

6. Until we are ready to give our all, if necessary to keep the church alive Mark 10:28.

REMEMBER, every member has a part to play in growing the church – first of all growing as a Christian and helping others to grow, then reaching out to the unsaved to share with them the salvation you enjoy. One may not be able to do it in the same way as someone else may do it, do what you can. (Remember to teach, encourage, be friendly, invite – be an example of a faithful Christian.)

There are probably some folks that only you can reach – your friend or neighbor down the street or on the next block.

Appeal – What is your standing with Christ today?

Are you a faithful worker? Are you a backslider? Are

you unsaved because you've never been introduced to CHRIST and His way of life?

JESUS came as GOD in the flesh. He bore the name JESUS because He was to save people from their sins. Matthew 1:21. He gave His life on a cross, thus becoming sin for us. GOD raised Him from the dead, and anointed Him, making Him both Lord and Christ.

In His death he purchased our redemption, even the forgiveness of our sins, Through His shed blood, he purchased a church, of which all men must be a member of to be saved. Upon obedience to the gospel, He adds us to the church where we take our place as workers til He comes again.

Believe the love story.

Turn your life over to Him through repentance and complete your obedience by being baptized – sins washed away, sins remitted, saved.

Part Four

This is the concluding lesson on this series of lessons on Church Growth Now. I believe it is the desire of every devoted Christian to see the Church grow spiritually and numerically. GOD wants it to grow, as every living thing is expected to grow. The church was designed to grow as shown by many of the parables that JESUS gave.

Spiritual growth must take top billing over numerical growth. (Swelling is from within and shows on the outside.) Few can accomplish great things if they aren't focused on the task at hand. Case of Gideon in his battles with the Midianites Judges 7:1–7; 16–23. Read that chapter for the entire story (may be some hard to pronounce names); preaching of the gospel to the world began with 12 men, (GOD working with them) and the mission was accomplished before the end of the 1st century. Colossians 1:23

GOD gives the victory, but only after the people do their part. Note 1 Corinthians 3:6.

The word of GOD is the primary element in Church growth. It is the seed of the Kingdom/Church. Growth – both spiritual and numerical have been presented over the past four lessons, however what you do with the essences of the lessons is up to you.

CHURCH GROWTH IN THE COMMUNITY

Introduction

1. A few months ago I was given a questionnaire designed to determine the relationship between the Church and the Community in which it exists. Some of the questions went something like this:

   a. What has been the historical role of the Church?

   b. Have the purpose and the function of the Church changed in the last few years?

   c. What amount of the budget is directed towards the needs of the community, etc.?

2. I believe the role of the Church is essentially the same as yesteryear. Maybe the scope has broadened, for with the passing of time, new ideas, new methods, new ways of accomplishing our goals, new ways have come about.

3. Truly the church must make its imprint upon the community. It must or should draw from the community in making up its membership. (This isn't always true.)

4. The community welcomes anything and everything. The church should take advantage of this and make its presence felt. The Church should be in the lead in

its given community. The Church cannot grow when it allows the community to set the light for it. (This happens so often.)

Whatever the world comes up with we readily accept. WHAT ARE WE OFFERING THOSE OF OUR COMMUNITY? What about the fads and styles of our day? The Church must set the light for the community and not the community for the Church.

5. The Church in Jerusalem grew because it was respected innate city. Acts 2:47

6. To make the influence of the Church felt in a community, the Church must show an interest, must become involved.

  a. That the material needs of the community are being met Sometimes we are the last to help and that should not be the case as is evidenced in Galatians 6:10.

  b. Things such as advice and practical guidance like scout troops, etc. Often people do not realize that all needs are not monetary, as evidenced with the need for guidance through the afore mentioned scout troop. (Acts 2:44)

  c. Spiritual instruction – CHRIST must be present to the area. This is done both by example and precept. Teaching and showing the community how to be neighborly. But teach them the truth, for only through obedience to the truth can they be added to the Church. Also, the primary interest of the gospel is spiritual. We must show more concern for, *"the world to come"* than *"this present world."* In all that the Church does, there must be desire to save the soul of man.

7. Let me add these few items of interest that might help the growth of the Church in a community:

   a. Mail out appropriate cards, letters to the sick, discouraged, new comers, newlyweds, new parents, bereaved, etc. and on special occasions to the permanent shut–ins and widows indeed.

   b. Commend police actions (*Thank them when a job is well done maybe by letter.*)

Conclusion

I believe when these things are followed, it will result in the Church being respected and many people (not all) becoming members of the Church that honors the CHRIST, Who died for it. 1 Thessalonians 1:4

What is your standing with CHRIST right now?
If you are a faithful worker, continue.

If you are a backslider, return.

If you've never obeyed the gospel, realize you're being robbed of life's greatest privilege and accept the invitation from the LORD and Church right now!

The Bible expresses social concern toward those around us. (Galatians 6:10; James 2:6; 5:4) Let's also be mindful of the attitude of the Good Samaritan in Luke 10:25–37 who seemed to operate under this motto, *"What is mine is yours and if you have a need, I will help you."*

The early Church manifested its interest in the needy and the destitute of its day. Acts 2:44; 4:32; 6:1–6; Romans 15:26–27. CHRIST was not unmoved by the hunger, sickness, and death He saw in the world, but this was not His chief concern. The Church is all sufficient as an institution in which and through which Christians can work toward carrying out the purpose of GOD. In all that the Church does, there must be the desire to save the soul of man.

DO ALL IN THE NAME OF THE LORD

To Preacher of this fine congregation, to any area church that might be present, to fellow proclaimers of the gospel of CHRIST, and friends who are fellow lovers of the truth. I am glad to be here tonight to fill my place on this lectureship program.

According to the theme of these discussions, we are informed that there is no condemnation to them who are in CHRIST JESUS. What the law (Law of Moses) could not do has been accomplished in CHRIST JESUS. However, to escape condemnation, we <u>must walk after the SPIRIT and not after the flesh</u>. The SPIRIT should dictate the course of our lives rather than the flesh. Galatians 5:16–26

My topic for tonight's discussion is, "Do All in the Name of LORD." Colossians 3:17 serves as the basis of this lesson. (*Quote this.*) These few words become the law of the kingdom of CHRIST. It is an advantage to have the laws of a kingdom as concise and in as few words as possible.

1. GOD gave the law to Israel in the Ten
   Commandments, and they were further reduced to
   two by JESUS – for the first four relate to GOD, the
   other six to man. Colossians 3:17 contains law of
   action for <u>every</u> word and deed, thought, place, and

circumstance.

"In His name" implies three things:
1. By His authority Acts 3:6–4:10
2. For His sake Mark 9:41; Matthew25:31 – a scene of Judgement and
3. For His glory Acts15:26 – Judas and Silas, men who hazarded their lives for the name of the LORD JESUS CHRIST.

This "law" put us on guard against doing things in our names or the names of the great among us. Acts 5:35 From just praising Him to suffering should be in the Name...etc. Why? His name is above every name. Ephesians 1:20–23; Philippians 2:9–11 For our benefit, let's go back to Colossians 3:1 and come down.

He is our mediator 1 Tim. 2:5 & book of Hebrews.

Note the teachings of JESUS according to Matthew 6:1–18; James 4:13–15.

To the unconverted, the LORD JESUS CHRIST has earned the right to expect you to obey him and then work through His name until the end of time.

GETTING READY FOR SPACE TRAVEL
1 Thessalonians 4:15–17; 5:23

A.

It is almost unbelievable the things we've seen in the past several years and promises for the future as it relates to space travel. Travel to various planets, space walks, etc. Before men are permitted to make a journey into space, they are required to undergo extensive preparation/training. The whole man (mind, emotions, and body) must be prepared.

1. Mind prepared with facts, both the ship and his surroundings. One unknown fact could mean the difference between life and death.

2. Emotions tested to see if they could live in close quarters for long periods of time. Could they live with each other under these circumstances? Their ability to make decisions traveling at 18,000 miles an hour. Would they be capable of doing the necessary things should something go wrong?

It also had to be determined in these conditions whether they were able to move around, eat sleep and handle the controls adequately. ALL of this has to be determined and the dangers removed before people are allowed to man a capsule into space.

B.

Application: the Bible in a sense proclaims every human being to be a spiritual prospect for space travel. It is essential, absolutely essential, that we prepare ourselves as we face eternity and anticipate space travel. whole spirit and soul and body– the mind must be in tune with the mind of GOD – accomplished by faith. The Scriptures tell us what one must believe, Mark 16:15–16; Romans 10:13.

The Gospel – not mere theory, no matter how plausible it may be; no human creeds, no matter how wise or spiritual the men who devise them; faith comes, but not miraculously, but when we hear, think, reason, understand and believe. Many fail to obey first principles.

GOD'S GRACE: PAST, PRESENT, AND FUTURE
Titus 2:11–14

THE GRACE OF GOD – Every blessing that has come to man since his beginning is from <u>Grace</u>. Grace, because man had not earned it. In the simple form, grace is unmerited favor. It is unconditional in that it is not hindered by sin, nor lack of works. Yet, grace is obliging and constraining (once received.) Without this effect, grace is received in vain.

In the Scripture, grace is connected with CHRIST because it is manifested through Him. In our text GRACE, as related to salvation, is applied as to distinction of time – past, present, and future. Past as it points to what has happened; present as to what is happening; and future as to what will happen.

PAST

It "hath appeared." This appearance was visible in that it appeared in human form. GOD sent us His Son to redeem/save mankind from its fallen and sinful state. Verse 13 refers to JESUS as our SAVIOR, and in v. 14, it says He "gave Himself for us!" As GOD and man, He exhibited selflessness and as a perfect sacrifice, offered Himself at/on the cross at Calvary. He was taunted and belittled, but for the joy set before Him, He endured the cross and despised the shame. (If you're The CHRIST/GOD's Son, come down.) The salvation made possible is within reach of all who comply with the terms required. Romans 1:14–16; Acts 10:34 (Men of all nations – rich or poor – high or low, etc. – *All Men*)

PRESENT

Grace, as a teacher, teaches us how we ought to live "in this present world." v. 12 The teaching is both negative and positive.

Negative – Denying ungodly and worldly lust. GOD's grace restrains, controls, and even chastises.

NOTE:

1: Lack of love, fear, and trust for/in GOD, and spirit of disobedience.

2. W. L. – corrupt/evil desires – things that satisfy only in this world. 1 John 215–17; chastening Hebrews 12:5–11.

Positive – Live soberly, righteously, and GODly having self-mastery, reverence toward GOD and respect for spiritual things. The gospel teaches every phase of life, whether toward self, our fellowman or our GOD. Acts 13:43; Hebrews12:15

FUTURE

"Looking for the blessed hope" etc. v. 13

Rest that awaits the people of GOD Hebrews 4:9; 2 Thessalonians 1:7

Those asleep in JESUS will be raised. John 11:25–26

Live in an environment where peace and love abides, where sin cannot invade. Revelation 21:1–8, 27. All of this will be accomplished at the SAVIOR's coming. Revelation 22:12

Conclusion

Are you ready for His coming? Preparation for His coming should/must be made now, on the basis of what was done in the past. JESUS made available a plan – Hear and Believe the gospel of CHRIST (based on His D.B.R.) Repent or turn to Him by a decision to forsake sin or anything that is contrary to His will; Be baptized to connect with salvation.

For Grace Is Undeserved Favor Shown Freely by/of the Goodness of Another

I've heard it said that there is not enough preaching about grace. If we know the meaning of grace, we will see GOD's grace when we see in the Bible where He makes a helpmeet for Adam; when he planted a garden for Adam's home; and in that garden He made to grow every tree that was pleasing to the sight and good for food; His dealings with Abraham, Isaac, and Jacob; and in JESUS's coming to pay the required debt for sin. John 3:16

The definition of grace is given in the title of this piece and whether the word, grace, is mentioned or not in the passages above, the very actions of GOD are a testimony of His grace. That's like the words "Trinity and Rapture," are not found in the Bible, but what they represent is taught.

JESUS had already introduced grace, even though He did not use the word grace. He pictured grace in all His actions and teachings: woman caught in the act of adultery John 8; raising of the widow's son Luke 7:11 (widow a mother – an only son); thief on the cross Luke 23:33, 39–43.

Grace is shown in Matthew 5:45 – sends rain on the unjust as well as the just; sun rises on the evil as well as the good; Luke 4:18,19 further expounds upon the fact that GOD sent JESUS to preach good news to the poor, heal the broken–hearted, preach deliverance to the captives, give sight to the blind, set at liberty them that are bruised, and preach the acceptable year of the LORD.

In the parables of JESUS, we can/do see the working of the grace of GOD, not sermons on it but stories about it.

1st Parable – The kingdom as a vineyard in Matthew 20, especially in the payoff section of the story. The owner of the vineyard gave equally to all who worked in His vineyard, whether they worked long or short. Those who worked all day questioned the generosity of the owner in verses 11 and 12. The owner's answer was given in verses 13–15.

People don't always like how GOD dispenses His grace. We think grace is only for those who are *good* and doing their very best, NOT for the rejects of society. Grace is designed to lift from the lower to the higher state of life. To us this may seem unfair, but grace is of GOD and He can/will dispense of it as He wills, without using our yardstick. (So often, we forget in our Christian walk that we are recipients of unmerited favor as well – the very definition of grace.) And too, we must remember that there is none good but The FATHER. Mark 10:18 And we must remember that JESUS, the Owner of the Church, will give eternal life to everyone who is a dedicated worker, regardless of the amount of time spent in service.

2nd Parable – Let us look at a story found in Luke 18:9–14. This is a story about two men who went to the temple to pray – one a Pharisee, the other a publican or a tax collector. Both surely expected blessings from GOD, but one went home justified rather than the other. In this, I drew a comparison between Saul/Paul (his life pre and post the Damascus Road) and the Pharisee and the publican. 1st man (Pharisee) who visited the temple with His confident, self–righteous attitude and 2nd man (publican, tax collector) with his recognition of his helpless, undone condition and his need of forgiveness. Saul/Paul in his pre-Damascus Road days, was more like the first man in our story to visit the temple (all arrogant, proud, boastful) but in 1 Corinthians 15:9–10, you can see an attitude shift where Paul writes, "*9 For I am the least of the apostles and do not even deserve to be called an apostle, because I persecuted the church of GOD. 10 But by the grace of GOD I am what I am, and His grace to me was not without effect. No, I worked harder than all of them— yet not I, but the grace of GOD that was in me.*"

The apostle Paul had such an attitude change that he used the word grace often in his writings – some 88 times. The word, grace, is used in all his 13 epistles. Usually, our teaching on the subject comes from the passages that Paul gives. This has been called, "*Getting at Grace Through the Back Door.*"

Whether Paul ever heard of this parable or not, it is a fitting biography of his own life.

As the Pharisee, at one time Paul had been so proud of himself, so confident of his own righteousness, and so sure GOD was pleased with him. He was trained at the feet of the best teacher in Israel; was advanced in the Jew's religion beyond many his own equal/age; was a rising star in his father's religion; he was as zealous for GOD as anyone – more than most. NOTE Gal.1:13–14; Philippians 3:4–6

There was a time when he would have thanked GOD, he

was not as other men were – robbers, adulterers, evil doers, etc. Thanked GOD, he was not a deluded or brainwashed Christian. He was proud to hold the coats of those who stoned Stephen and was eager to persecute this new sect. But after that Damascus Rd. trip, he was never the same.

GOD saw a man in need of grace and got his attention by a blinding light; JESUS, the LORD, talked with him; he forgot his intended mission and spent three days fasting and praying – a time of grieving, repentance and remorse. For the first time in his life, Paul felt like a tax collector – no good deeds to boast of; no righteousness to trust in; no–one to compare himself to and feel better.

For the first time in his life, the man who had pounded his chest, is now beating his breast, and crying out, "GOD be merciful – forgive me – I'm a sinner." Paul knows, at last, that a right relationship with GOD is founded in the unexplainable, unimaginable, amazing grace of GOD. All he once was proud of is now garbage. All that had filled him with confidence and self–praise is now dung.

GOD sent Ananias to him to restore his sight, that he might be filled with the Holy Ghost, and to assist him in obeying the principles of the gospel. Paul was baptized to have his sins washed away.

GRACE AND ITS DEMANDS

In this study, I want to further show that grace does not relieve us of our responsibilities. This is a fact that many don't understand. They look at grace only as, "It saves from sin, but if it obligates you or changes you, that's not grace." Questions are asked:

What good is grace if it means you have to take up a cross and follow JESUS?

What good is grace if you still have to die to yourself, to sin, and the world?

What good is grace if instead of freeing you to live as you please, it makes you the love–slave of the one who has been gracious to you?

Remember the people in Paul's day who misunderstood grace. The Romans thought they could sin because they were not under the law, but under grace. Romans 5; the Corinthians were boasting because one in their number was living with his father's wife. Maybe they thought this is what grace is all about. It's okay because GOD is a gracious GOD.

Paul corrected them when he said, "It is for freedom that CHRIST has set us free." But note the warning that follows, "Don't use your freedom as an excuse to indulge the sinful nature." Galatians 5

And there are still those today who want grace free from all demands. People are eager to be forgiven, but not quite ready to be transformed. We want GOD's gifts but resent having to respond to GOD's grace. We want grace without obligation, a grace without holiness, a grace without having to be involved in kingdom business, a grace that saves us and leaves us alone.

In religion people are constantly searching for the place where grace is to be obtained at the cheapest price. The grace JESUS talked about is not the same thing that people pass off as grace today. The JESUS grace, not only saves us, it changes us. True grace, truly received, always makes a genuine difference in our lives. It either changes us completely or condemns us completely; it either transforms us or destroys us. The grace of JESUS gives everything, but it demands everything, as well; it is free, but it is never cheap. In our text, Matthew 18:21–35, we have a story of grace received. One view of the story presses the need to forgive each other. Note – The two verses preceding our lesson text where Peter asked about forgiveness and the text closes with forgiveness from GOD. Verse 35

A second view shows the grace of GOD bestowed on us and the demand it places upon us.

1. Man brought before the king who owed an unimaginable sum of money – millions, the earnings

of a thousand lifetimes.

2. Demand for payment, (in other words, pay me what you owe me) but of course the man couldn't pay.

3. Command to sell him, his wife, his wife, children and all of his possessions, that some payment might be made.

4. Plea for mercy (humble plea) – the man fell down and worshipped him saying, "Lord, have patience with me and I will pay thee all." The unimaginable happens – the king's heart is touched and with pity and mercy, he forgives the servant the whole amount owed him. GRACE!

Some would stop the story here, thus freeing the receiver of grace from **any** obligations. GOD has done for us what the king did for that servant. As sinners, we could not repay our debt – remove the penalty of sin. GOD took pity upon us and sent His Son to pay the price. In Him we have redemption, even the forgiveness of sins, and that according to the presence of His **grace**. Sometimes we want to stay in the throne room and not worry about what comes next. We want the gift without bothering to consider its implications, **but** the story doesn't end here. Notice the action of the forgiven servant.

1. He found a fellow–servant who owed him a hundred

pence – lunch money.

2. His demand, which he had a right to do though maybe wrong in the way he approached him – (same thing the king had done), but the servant couldn't pay.

3. This servant fell at his creditor's feet and begs for mercy – be patient...I will repay thee all (same thing he had said).

4. The unimaginable happens – Had no mercy – threw him in prison until he should pay the debt. He who had just come from the throne room where he was given grace, shown mercy, yea forgiven all his debt, how could he be so hard–hearted? How could he refuse to show pity and mercy toward his fellow servant? **He forgave nothing!**

Grace should have changed him, made a difference in the way he acted and felt. Grace required that he should start acting more like his king.

So, the End of the Story (Verses 31–34) – The story ends back in the throne room.

1. 2nd incident reported

2. 1st servant called back and was addressed as a "wicked" servant, not because he requested payment from his fellow servant, but because he had not allowed the king's grace to change him, in other

words, because the king's grace had not convinced him to act more like his king.

Grace given is expected to result in graciousness. Grace demands a change. You just don't remain the same. The wickedness of the servant stirred the anger of the king, and the servant was turned over to the jailers to be tortured 'til he should pay all he owed. (The family was exempted on this score.) GRACE!

Where grace makes no difference, it is revoked. While this parable may be called, "The unmerciful Servant," it might well be called the unchanged servant. Those who don't understand that grace demands a change, have no real understanding of grace. It changes our lifestyle – so can't take sin lightly, ignore holiness as if it were optional, nor trifle with temptation. It changes us when it comes to involvement – can't be just spectators and not workers.

Many leave the throne room just as obsessed and just as consumed with their own business as when they came in. It's easy to belong to the church if you never inconvenience yourself with what's going on where involvement is confined to Sunday morning worship, no teaching, no worry about reaching the lost or encouraging the downhearted. If grace doesn't make you love the work of GOD, the people of GOD and the plan of GOD, you don't really understand grace. It changes us as relating to discipleship. Some have concluded that because of grace, all that stuff about denying self, taking up the cross and following where JESUS leads, all that stuff about walking in His steps; all that stuff about living the life that JESUS lived is a bunch of baloney. But remember, when we leave the throne room of forgiveness, the rest of our lives is to be lived in gratitude to the One who showed us His grace.

Where do you stand in regard to GOD's grace?

THE CULMINATION OF
THE TREATISE ON GRACE
Matthew 25:14

The first story of grace in this portion of the treatise on grace is found in Matthew 22:1–14 and is about a king who prepares a marriage feast for his son. This is a kingdom parable that teaches many lessons, with grace being one of the outstanding ones.

As the story goes…
1. A guest list had been drawn up, maybe of the upper-class people and invitations had been sent.
2. Meal was prepared and no pain nor expense was spared.
3. When all was ready, servants were sent out to let the guests know, "Now is the time – all things are ready."
4. The special guests "would not come."
5. The king sends other servants to them to explain to them how much expense he had gone to, so "would they please come?"
6. They made light of it (*not worth considering and can feast at home*) and went their own ways – their personal pursuits and interests.

7. The king judged them unworthy and destroyed them, so they are eliminated from the feast.

8. The invitation to the feast is extended to anyone who may be found (highways, byways, hedges, poor, maimed, halt and blind) Verse 10 says both good and bad were brought.

9. When the king came in, he saw a man among them which had not on a wedding garment. Upon being questioned, the man could not answer. At the king's request the man was bound and cast into outer darkness. And the story closes with, "For many are called, but few are chosen."

Application

The king must be GOD, Who by His grace, has prepared the gospel as a great feast for mankind. This is because Jesus Christ, the Bridegroom, (His Son) Who came to earth to save man, and in the process became espoused to His bride, the Church.

The first invitation was sent to the Jews, whom GOD favored through the years. BUT they refused. "Felt they were better than what was being offered.

The Limited Commission was to the Jews only. (Matthew 10:5–6) Seventy were also sent under this Commission and when it was extended to all men, Jews still had the first chance. (Jerusalem, Judea, Samaria) uttermost parts of the earth. Acts 13:46 "The first shall be last and the last shall be first."

To those who had been the betrayers and murderers of JESUS, GOD extended grace. Let's look again at the three kinds of guests of the parable.

Those who flatly refused the king's invitation.

Those who accepted it even though they were unworthy.

The one man who proved unworthy even–though he attended the feast.

These three are represented today, even as the invitation goes out to all.

1. Those who flatly refused. How many today hear the king's invitation to the feast, but decide not to come? (Too busy; self–satisfied; self–sufficient.) Happy with their food and their garments. (I'm good enough.) So people are still making excuses. If pressed, these people can/do become downright violent. Beware. Refusal of grace today may mean no grace tomorrow! GOD can be severe.

2. Those who have accepted the invitation, even though they may not have passed man's test of worthiness. (*They're too bad.*) With GOD, it doesn't matter how bad a person is, He can clean

you up and dress you out in a rich robe – make you ready to sit at the king's table, effective through obedience to the gospel. Romans 6:17–18; 1–6; Acts 2:26–38; Galatians 3:26–27; 2 Corinthians 5:17

Each of us can ask: when I received GOD's invitation, what was my condition when I arrived at the door? Thanks be to GOD that He gave me new clothes and a second chance.

3. Those who hear the invitation, come to the feast, but think they can sit at GOD's table in their own filthy rags. They refuse the offer of new clothes. I was invited like this and I see no need to change. So, they sit there proud, stubborn, unchanged and unmoved by the grace of GOD. One day, GOD will demand an answer, as to why we aren't properly dressed. NOTE Revelation 19:7–9

Those who refuse GOD's grace or abuse it will be denied the privilege of attending the marriage of the LAMB in the afterwhile.

Another lesson comes to us from Matthew 25:14, which tells of a man traveling to a far country, but before leaving, he called unto him his servants and delivered unto them his goods. To one he gave five talents; to another he gave two; to

another he gave one. A talent of gold was said to be worth
30,000 dollars and of silver it valued 2,000 dollars. Later, in
Palestine it was worth about 560 dollars. Either multiplied by
5 or 2 would run from 150,000 dollars/60,000 dollars to
2,800 dollars or 1,120 dollars.

This story is not just about money or earthly masters – it
is an allegory for GOD's kingdom and the manner in which
GOD deals with each of us. The graciousness of GOD is seen
in the Master Who freely gave "all his goods" into the hands
of his servants. He didn't have to – he could have invested it
himself, but he believed in his servants and as an act of faith,
he untrusted his money to them. Everything we have, GOD
gave it to us. He gave to each servant only what he had the
ability to do. Nothing is burdening them down and there were
no impossible demands nor unrealistic expectations.

Graciousness shown in the treatment of the two servants
who had put the money to exchange (even at risk) and
increased the master's holdings. Another side of the
Master/GOD is apparently presented at the end of the story.

In all this we see grace extended, grace rewarded and
grace's limits. Let's take a look at the three servants.

To them their lord was a good man, a generous man, a
man whom they loved rather than feared. They believed that
when the lord returned, no matter how well or how poorly
they had done, their lord could be counted on to deal with

them in a gracious manner. And in fact, he did treat them graciously. Verse 21, 22, 23

Few – many: enter the joys.

This parable of the kingdom deals with those in the kingdom, the Church. Others have dealt with an invitation to souls to come. **Those in**, be thankful for the grace that has brought you as far as you are and trust grace to carry you on. Those outside, grace is extended to you! Won't you **ACCEPT**?

Last Parable and Conclusion of this Treatise on Grace

For our last parable on grace, let's look at the story of a father and two sons as found in Luke 15:11–32. The story begins with the father dividing up his savings among his sons and that done freely and without hesitation. Like GOD, he is glad to give good gifts to his children. The younger son took his portion of goods and went away to a far country (far from home), and there wasted his fortune in wild living, (*did just what he wanted to do*). This was an abuse of his father's gift and his father's trust. His actions caused him to hit "rock bottom." When he had spent all, famine came, and he began to be in "want." He had no money, no food, nobody hiring, so he had to take what he could get – feeding swine.

He does come home, but why? He's hungry! He thinks of his father's servants, who had bread enough and to spare.

Note: His return and the attitude with which he comes. Verse 18–21. He exemplifies humility; realized what he had done and confessed it.

The father – the most important character of the story represents GOD, the Giver of grace. When the younger son returns, the father saw him "a great way off" and ran and fell on his neck and kissed him. Verse 20 He interrupts the confession, not with, "I told you so," nor "laying down conditions for his coming home," but with love, joy, and relief, saying to the servants…verse 22–24. GRACE! The boy got more than he expected and maybe far more than he deserved.

I'd like to think that the son may have made a complete change because of this "second grace." Hopefully, he was ever grateful and stayed close to his father from then on. (The Bible doesn't say.)

Now, the older son – verse 25–30 was no better than the younger one, for even though he had stayed at home, in heart and/or attitude, he too, was in a far country. A self–righteous attitude kept him from rejoicing at the return of his brother. Whereas the humility of the younger son kept him recognizing that all he was, and had, was because of the goodness/graciousness of his father.

We see the comparison between him and his brother. Verse 29–30 "I'm the good one." "Thy son," a worthless, wasteful whoremonger... "You never gave me a party. But for your no good son, you've killed the fatted calf."

The gracious father doesn't scold for his oldest son's lack of understanding or sympathy, but rather reasons with him. Vs 31–32 You've always been here and what was mine was yours. I didn't know you wanted or needed a party. But as for thy brother (not just my son) he was gone, and we didn't know where he was or if he would ever return. It is right that we welcome him back with gladness and merriment. He was dead (same as) and is alive again; he was lost and is found.

Grace is reaching out to those who least deserve it. Note the purpose of the parable, 15:1–2. GOD's grace extends to all – He would have all men saved and come to the knowledge of the truth. In salvation, there is always GOD's part and man's part. Ephesians 2:8,9.

Wrap Up

I'm sure enough has been said about grace that those who have read thus far have gotten a clear vision of true grace. Grace is nothing new, for it has been in action since the dawn of time through extended ages. Man is saved from sin brought on by Adam. Yes, man is saved by the grace/free gift of GOD, through JESUS CHRIST. That act does not give us license to keep sinning in hope of more grace. People are eager to be forgiven, but not quite ready to be transformed. In other words, we want grace without obligation.

Grace affects people in different ways. Tim Woodruff describes it as the reaction one gets in kicking a rock or a dog. A rock has no energy – it's not active but acted upon. (It only acts to the force applied to it.) Kick it and it rolls; drop it and it falls; hit it and it shatters. However, kicking a dog is something altogether different. A dog has the ability to transform energy. The energy from the foot brings back a snarling, snapping rage that signals attack. A dog is not passive; he has an energy of his own. Your energy applied to a dog may get more energy back than expected or wanted.

For application, we react to GOD's grace (his goodness) either as a Rock or a Dog. For some, religion, salvation, even church going gets no positive response. They don't allow worshipping and serving GOD to lead them to a greater love and appreciation of GOD's goodness. To them, it is a bore to go to church, (sing the same old songs, see the same old folks, hear the same old sermons, etc.) They, like a rock, are kicked, but they don't kick back. BUT...

The Christian religion can be dog–like – knowing what GOD has done and is doing for us should cause us, by faith, to kick back with a joy unspeakable, with gratitude and love. Let each of us examine ourselves and see where we fit in in this rock–dog like experience.

Remember, grace is a way of life, not just a point of doctrine. It's with us and around us at all times. Lastly, let's remember that all of us are who we are and what we are by the grace of GOD. As the saying goes, we are here, not because we've been so good… the extension of time is a matter of GOD's grace. 2 Peter 3:9

How Long the Night?
Psalm 30:5

At some points in life, a minute can seem like an hour, an hour can seem like an eternity. Every day seems endlessly stormy and every night knows no end to the depths of its darkness. This is when we are reminded of the words of David, "Weeping may endure for a night, but joy cometh in the morning." (*It will be better in the morning.*) These words seem appropriate for a man who had been in battle with a bear; who had taken on the Philistine giant, Goliath, singlehandedly; one who while being intensely loyal to his master, the king, was the target of intense hate; one who had countless enemies, but still had a friend; one who had already been to hell a hundred times, but still had a hope of heaven; one who deserved the anger of GOD, but had come to know GOD's sure mercies.

Probably because of the things just mentioned, the text has become a panacea for a man's ills; his hope in hopeless situations. Surely, we all have our nights or have had. Somebody has a secret you haven't told anybody today because it is night. Some of us are still waiting for the dawn of morning, while others have experienced the morning and its joys.

Now, some of you probably think the preacher shouldn't have any nights. Sometimes it seems the older I get, the longer and longer my nights become. And even–though I look the same and act the same, there is often a darkness that prevents me from seeing the light at the end of the tunnel. Many times, I wonder, "how..."

Speaking of the night, it is interesting to note the many instances in the Bible that took place at night. It was night when Jacob wrestled with the angel; ten plagues visited upon Egypt; Belshazzar and handwriting; prayer meeting of church for Peter: Paul and Silas prayed at night in prison.

JESUS hung on the cross on Friday and even though the clock of time said 3o'clock in the afternoon, the clock of eternity said it was midnight. For we are told that the sun refused to shine. And when the sun doesn't shine, it's night.

In the midst of, or along with, our personal nights, bring this thought more into focus: be reminded that it is night socially, morally, and spiritually.

1. Socially as the gap between the "haves" and the "have nots" is widening; where caste and class are being reinstituted; where the economics of this "insanity" system is presided over by the highest officials of our land. They no longer keep children out of schools by legislation but legislate to keep them too poor to attend. We are living in

a social night when the meaning of poverty is being redefined daily. There was a time if you made 10 or 15 thousand a year, you were somebody. Now, this amount is considered the poverty level.

2. Morally – <u>A night</u> which has seen the line between right and wrong erased. <u>A night</u> which says marriage is a thing of the past and home is where your hat and toothbrush is. <u>A night</u> where the end of life is to get high by any and every means available. <u>A night</u> where traditional values are gone, children are telling their parents what to do and parents are afraid of the children they feed and clothe. DON'T LOOK NOW, BUT IT'S NIGHT!

3. Spiritually – The deepest night in my soul is when I realize that church is not church like it used to be. There's something unsettling in church when people would rather applaud than say amen. There is something spiritually wrong when churches spend more time in planning picnics and parties than they do in praying in prayer meetings. Also when people lose interest when fun time isn't provided, that is part of spiritual night. There is something spiritually wrong when

folk can sit three hours in a style show at a ball game, before a TV, but can't sit 45 minutes through a sermon without thinking, "It's too much church." There is something spiritually wrong when folk take time allotted to GOD to prepare/enjoy a big meal with family and friends rather than meet the LORD in the assemblies and feast on His word or around His table. Something's wrong where our worldly knowledge increases and spiritual knowledge decreases. ~IT'S NIGHT~

Personally, socially, morally and spiritually, it's night and I am just asking, "How long the night!"

I know there's a better day coming, but how long the night?

I know GOD moves in mysterious ways His wonders to perform, but how long the night?

I know, "All things work together for good for those who love the LORD," but how long the night?

I know I need to "Wait on the LORD and be of good courage," but...?

I know He knows how much I can bear, but how long the night?

I know there's a bright side somewhere, but how long

the night?

I/you/we can know that the longer the night, the less time we have to wait.

As we endure, and indeed we must, the night we need a power outside ourselves and stronger than ourselves to succor us. The LORD is that Power. Philippians 4:12, 2 Corinthians 12:8, Isaiah 23

Accept Him and dwell with Him!

MECHANICAL INSTRUMENTAL MUSIC

To use or not to use in worship to GOD, has been an ongoing debate for centuries. Presently, it is being discussed between the church of CHRIST and the Christian Church. According to published reports, a few churches of CHRIST have added the instrument to their worship, resulting in two worship services, one for those who contend for the old order and one for the more progressive.

In the mid–19th century, the instrument (a piano) was introduced into the COC resulting in a split that led to the establishment of the Christian Church. The COC of the old order still objects and rejects the use of mechanical instruments in worship. Why?

My explanation begins with saying, there is no N.T. authority for its use. As the head of the church, JESUS alone can dictate policy. He did not command it; the apostles sent for did not teach it or practice it; the Holy Spirit was to bring to their remembrance what CHRIST taught them **and** guide them into all truths. Also, the early church continued steadfastly in the apostles' doctrine. (Acts 2:42)

When the church was under the direct guidance of the SPIRIT, the mechanical instrument is not found. (The O.T. is full of the names of instruments and their use in praise to

GOD. But not a single one is mentioned in connection with worship in the N.T.) The worship of the N.T. consists of singing, praying, communion, teaching and giving.

Church at Corinthians 14 – chapter dealing with unknown tongues and their use in worship verse 23 – whole chapter, etc.; verse 15 – singing and praying; verse19 – speaking words of understanding that people may be taught.

Church at Ephesus – as related to church music, Ephesians 5:19

Church at Colosse – Colossians 3:16

Hebrews Christians – Hebrews 2:11–12, 13:15

Conclusion

Doctrine of CHRIST 2 John 9

Follow what is in it – reject what isn't there. It might be fair to ask those who use the instruments to tell why they use them. The answers might be many, but not because the New Testament commands it.

Arguments for Its Use:

1. David used it – He's not the head of the church. In fact, he died before it was established. (Also, he did a lot of other things.)
2. Music will be in Heaven.
3. Worship is dead without it – depends upon where you

are and what you put into it.

4. It's an aid – may be more an addition.

5. "Psallo."

THE HEALING OF THE TEN LEPERS

Luke 17:11–19

Verses 11–14

On His way to Jerusalem, JESUS passed through the midst of Samaria and Galilee on the line that separated the 2 cities. As He went through (in a certain village) He met ten men that were lepers. O.T. gives an idea of what the disease is like – a most horrible and dreaded disease. (Comments of Albert Barnes in his discussion of Matthew 8.) A disease that separates a person from family and society. Our text says the men "stood afar off." The closest thing to this disease we can think of is AIDS – dread, fear, shun.

TOGETHER, they lifted their voices and said, JESUS, MASTER, have mercy on us. The cry was universal and earnest. Their cry was an expression of faith in the great physician, CHRIST.

Affliction often causes people to turn to GOD, but in the times of health and prosperity, many forget GOD.

Laodiceans

Knowing that one of these was a Samaritan, this shows that there are some things that reduce all men to one common level. This situation is probably the only thing that could cause a Jew and a Samaritan to be in the same crowd. Afflictions, tragedies, etc. have a way of erasing color (black or white), wealth (rich or poor), education (learned or ignorant), etc. They were all unclean and they all cried for mercy!

Sin makes all men unclean in the sight of the LORD and all men must look to GOD for mercy and forgiveness. Romans 3:9–23 when JESUS saw them, He said, "Go show thyself to the priest." Matthew 8

The priest was to give a letter of testimony of the fact that the leper was now clean and could be received again into his family, the congregation, and society in general. NOTE: JESUS told them to go as if the healing was already done (knowing it would be done.) This called for a strong faith – to go with nothing to show. But on faith they obeyed the command of JESUS and "As they went, they were cleansed." They were saved while in the act of obedience, not before nor after!" Go…" "As they went." SIMPLE? Yes! But still had to obey. So SINNERS defiled with the leprosy of sin must put faith in the LORD Jesus Christ and obey His commands, having the fullest confidence that He is able to and will heal if they follow His directions.

We should also be reminded that in bestowing His grace, GOD is no respecter of persons. Titus 2:11 (ALL MEN)

Verses 15–19

Ten healed but only ONE of them…turned back and with a loud voice glorified GOD. **The voice of prayer became the voice of praise** and <u>both</u> were with a <u>loud</u> voice. He was grateful for his healing because it had given him a new lease on life so he returned to thank the LORD. This he did before completing his journey – before receiving his papers.

And he was a Samaritan v. 16 – an element of surprise.

Man considered peculiarly wicked had drifted from GOD's original order of things. Called a stranger in verse 18 – foreigner, an alien or a man of another tribe, one of a foreign people. A man least expected to express this gratitude to GOD. Many from whom you expect nothing, often do and give the most, like the Good Samaritan of Luke 10. On the other hand, many of whom you expect the most often do the least or nothing. JESUS' final words to him, v. 19.

One of the blackest and ugliest sins of today is the sin of ungratefulness. Man ought not pray in time of distress only to be negligent in showing our gratefulness by being silent when thanks are in order.

Conclusion

    1. From the ten we learn that all need cleansing and can be cleansed.

2. From the one we learn the duty and beauty of thankfulness and only a few take time to thank GOD.

3. From the nine we learn that ingratitude is a very ugly sin and maybe GOD expects thanks.

4. For our Consideration:

   a. When the disciples meet for worship, where are the nine? When the church assembles on Sunday night, where are the nine?

   b. For prayer meetings and classes, where are the nine?

   c. In soul–winning campaigns, where are the nine?

   d. When the collection baskets are passed, where are the nine?

You have been cleansed by CHRIST; count your many blessings and name them one by one.

MARRIAGE

Marriage is what we often call a Holy Estate – for GOD ordained it so that man would not be alone, as the only kind of his species on the earth. GOD took a part of man and made him a woman and presented her unto him as a helpmeet. It was said, "Therefore shall a man leave his father and his mother and shall cleave unto his wife, and they shall be one flesh." Genesis 2.

Marriage under GOD begins with a civil or religious ceremony, giving testimony to the fact that two persons (man and woman – Adam and Eve not Adam and Steve) have mutually agreed to live together as husband and wife – with the intent of fulfilling all the following responsibilities:

Procreation.

Provision for sexual gratification and regulation.

Care of children and their education, etc.

The marriage under GOD is not to be confused with the practice of common–law–marriage, a union between a man and a woman that is made "outwardly" to appear like a marriage, but in which the parties do not have the intention "really" to be married to each other. The relationship is concubinage (living with a man on the basis of a position that is less than that of a wife.) This type of marriage is not sanctioned by GOD. 1 Corinthians 7:1–5; Hebrews13:4. No woman has the duty of a wife to perform, but she who is a wife; no man has the duty of a husband to perform, but he who is a husband.

Marriage is a serious step to take in life and the first thing you should consider in reference to it is, are you ready? This is a serious question because it involves current and future happiness. It takes more than being old enough to marry to be ready for it and it takes more than having the desire for marriage to be ready to enter into it.

You should not run into marriage just because people think it is time, a person seems to be a good catch, etc. (1986. Jack Wilhelm. RSVP NEWSLETTERS 219–01–86–51)

When you marry you are selecting a mate for life, so you need to look at the personality traits of a perspective spouse. There have been so many marriages that landed on the rocks because some marriage partners thought prior to the marriage, "I can change him/her, etc." *Note:* You have to be careful about planning to change anyone after your marriage because when a person is trying to get you, they will often hide certain character traits until after the marriage.

Then often the real person comes out: for example, if a person is selfish before you marry them, then look for them to be even more so afterwards. All of us have probably heard a heartbroken spouse say things like, "He/she has changed because they surely were not like that when I married them."

Finding the right mate may be somewhat unique in our day, but probably more difficult than in the ancient times of the patriarchs. Back then, families usually took the lead in searching out the right mate for their children. (Abraham, Rebekah, Isaac) Fathers could or could not give their consent for their daughters to be married. It might be well today, to consider the thinking of your family/families because whether you think so or not, you **ARE marrying The Family**.

Next to the decision to live for CHRIST comes the decision regarding the one you are going to marry. A wrong choice can tragically wreck your entire Christian life. On the other hand, the right choice can promise that your future years will be a bit of heaven on earth.

TO FIND THE RIGHT MATE

1. Seek GOD's help. His wisdom is always 24k.
2. If you are a Christian, then you should seek a Christian mate. Both are pulling together (think alike) not one bringing in and the other carrying out. Pray together, etc. (in view of children)
3. If you plan to marry a Christian, don't marry on a promise "to become." If he/she is baptized upon insistence, observe him/her for a time before

marrying him/her.

Especially to the Young Ladies

The truly important characteristics of a future husband is not in the way he combs/wears his hair or whether he has a car or not or how he polishes it. Instead, you need to look for the following attributes:

1. What inner qualities does he possess?
2. Is he thoughtful and kind?
3. Is he industrious or lazy?
4. Is he consistent? Does he keep his word?
5. How does he treat his parents? Gentle and respectful?
6. Does he like children, even his own brothers and sisters?
7. What about the compatibility of his and your likes and dislikes?
8. How do you get along when expressing opinions?
9. Look for someone who will provide for you.

Especially to the Young Men

Don't make the mistake of the fellow who fell in love with a "dimple," and then like a fool, he married the whole girl.

1. Can she cook?
2. Does she like children?

3. Can she sew?

4. Is she intelligent, having a passable education? (My girl couldn't spell "the.")

5. How does she treat her family?

6. Is she neat, faithful, considerate?

7. Seek a helper, someone who can manage.

Don't date anyone you would not want to marry. Is this the person you want for the father/mother of your children? What does he/she stand for? What about their past? A person's past doesn't always make the future wrong, but wrong without a manifested change can wreck a marriage. Remember, no going into a marriage thinking, "I'll change them later."

On how many things do you agree?

These are the principles that make for a happy marriage and cause you to heir together in eternal life.

Marriage needs to be a triangle, with CHRIST as the 3rd point. Obey Him today. The secret of marriage is commitment.

<u>Marriage Ceremony Example 1</u>

<u>Prelude</u>
<u>LIGHT CANDLES</u>
<u>SEAT MOTHERS</u>

<u>PROCESSIONAL</u>

Preacher, Groom and Best Man

Groomsmen and Bridesmaids

Ring Bearer and Flower Girl

Maid of Honor

Bride and Father – Audience Stand
(Please Be Seated)

Lighting of Victor's Candle by Bride

Prayer

Opening Statement: Michael Q. Groom and Myra G. Bride have come this afternoon to be joined in marriage.

Assembled here in this place of worship, standing here before GOD and these your relatives and friends as witnesses, let me remind you of the seriousness of marriage; it is as old as the family of man, with GOD as the author. In the book of beginnings, Genesis 2:18–25 we read that marriage is the older of GOD's two great institutions on earth – the home and the church. JESUS both beautified and adorned the institution of marriage by attending a wedding in Cana of Galilee, where He performed His first miracle – turning water into wine. He also taught the permanency of marriage when in discussion with the people of His day. Note: Matthew 19:3–6. The apostle declared it to be honorable in all and used it to describe the mystical union that exists between CHRIST and His church. (Ephesians 5:22–33)

In view of these facts, none of us can doubt its authority or seriousness and they should give us to know that marriage is not to be entered into thoughtlessly, lightly, or irreverently.

If anyone present has a just cause why these two people should not be joined in marriage, speak now or forever hereafter hold your peace.

I charge and require you both, if either of you know any reason why you should not be joined together, do now confess it; for all who are joined together other than GOD's word doth allow, are not joined together lawfully, nor is their union blessed of GOD.

WHO GIVE THIS WOMAN TO BE MARRIED TO THIS MAN?

Father gives bride a kiss and takes his seat.

Michael, do you take this woman to be your wife, to live with her and cherish her, to love honor and protect her, according to the ordinance of GOD?

Myra, do you take this man to be your husband, to live with him and cherish him, love him and honor him according to the ordinance of GOD?

EXCHANGE OF RINGS: The RING was used by Kings of old to sign various writs and documents. Today, it is used to seal this marriage vow. It is a symbol of marriage in at least two ways: the purity of gold symbolizes the purity of your love, AND the unending circle symbolizes the unending vows you are taking. Place the ring on her finger and repeat after me – "With this ring, etc." (First to groom and then to bride).

FINAL VOWS: Michael, take Myra's right hand and repeat after me, "I Michael Q. Groom take thee, Myra G. Bride to be my wedded wife, to have and to hold from this day forward, richer or for poorer, in sickness and in health and forsaking all others, I promise to keep myself wholly unto thee, so long as we both shall live." THEN Myra–

PRONOUNCEMENT: in as much as Michael and Myra have consented together in holy wedlock, witnessing the same before GOD and this congregation and sealing the same with the giving and receiving of a ring, by the power vested in me as a minister of the gospel of CHRIST and according to the laws of the state of Tennessee, I now pronounce you husband and wife.

(*Soft music*)

LIGHTING OF THE UNITY CANDLE: to my left, we have three candles, two of which are lighted. They represent Michael and Myra as they came here today – single, two separate individuals. I ask them to extinguish the two and light the candle in the center. This says that they are no more two but one – one in purpose, in dreams and aspirations.

Tribute to Mothers

Blessing of the marriage: prayer and reading of numbers 6:24–26 the Lord bless thee and keep thee: the Lord make his face shine upon thee and be gracious unto thee: the Lord lift his countenance upon thee and give thee peace.

You may now kiss the bride!

Kiss

Ladies and gentlemen, I now present to you Mr. and Mrs. Michael Q. Groom

AFTER THE WEDDING PARTY HAS MARCHED OUT, ANNOUNCE The receiving line is now forming in the foyer. You are now dismissed; go by and greet the wedding party.

Marriage Ceremony Example 2

Renewal of Marriage Vows
<u>Michael Q.</u> and <u>Myra G. Husband</u>

Have consented to renew their marriage vows after <u>50</u> years of marriage.

They have lived up to the vows that were exchanged, viz. taking each other to live after GOD's holy ordinances as related to marriage. Through their years of adjustment, good years and lean years – years, no doubt filled with both joys and sorrows, they have not forgotten their original vows – I take thee to be my lawful wedded wife, to love, honor and protect, through any and all adversity until death do we part. OR I take thee to be my lawful wedded husband, to love honor and obey, with the understanding that whither thou goest, I will go and where thou lodgest, I will lodge, until death do we part.

Certainly, your love for each other has grown through the years and you have brought a lot of happiness to each other. Out of this loving association, you have been given children, grandchildren, and great grandchildren. (*Add quantities and names, as requested by the couple.*)

As you are about to renew your vows, may you be reminded of the words of Paul in Corinthians 7:3–5 and

Ephesians 5:22–23.

Living by these principles will assure you happiness for the years ahead and will insure as per the words of Peter, that you will be <u>heirs together</u> of the grace of life.

JOIN HANDS AS YOU NOW RENEW YOUR VOWS

Upon the strength of your life of marriage for the past <u>50</u> years, do you <u>Michael O. Husband</u> promise to continue your life together as husband and wife, accepting your responsibilities as a husband, etc., for another <u>50</u> years or for as long as you shall live?

AND do you, <u>Myra G. Husband</u> promise to continue your life together, accepting your responsibilities as a wife (etc.) for another <u>50</u> years or for as long as you shall live?

ANY EXCHANGE OF TOKENS

In as much as this couple has just now renewed their marriage vows, before GOD and these witnesses, I now pronounce upon them the benediction of Numbers 6:24–26.

May your life be one of continued happiness and prosperity.

PRAYER and KISS

"The LORD bless thee and keep thee: The LORD make His face to shine upon thee and be gracious to thee: The LORD lift up His countenance upon thee and give thee peace."

I'm Married, Now What?

Your marriage needs to be worked at. Someone once said that good Christian homes are <u>made</u> in <u>Heaven</u> but come in a do-it-yourself kit, to be put together <u>on earth</u>. To build a marriage and avoid a divorce there must be:

1. A TOTAL COMMITTMENT to JESUS! See Luke 14:26.

2. Commitment to the Relationship. This commitment must be pre–eminent to all other relationships – parents, friends, children.

a. May not feel the same every day but remember there is a relationship to which you must be committed. Also, you must accept the whole package – good and bad – virtues and faults. (Like buying a record)

3. Commitment to Humble Service. Stubbornness, and pride is destructive; be subjected one to the other – Hannah and Elkanah

This kind of couple can be a true representative of CHRIST and His Church and become heirs together of the grace of life in the end.

Remember, it's all about the commitment.

OTHER SHEEP I HAVE

John 10:16

Introduction

CHRIST and His followers are compared to many things, but probably none of greater tenderness than the one of John 10. Here is a picture of a good Shepherd and His sheep. Following several observations, JESUS announces, "and other sheep I have", etc.

This is a misunderstood and misused passage, perhaps used in an effort to justify denominationalism. (Many churches today.) And rather than give them up, people use passages like this to justify their remaining in them. Mark 9:38.

The truth of the passage, John 10:16, can be understood only as we consider the WHOLE of the verse. The first part of the passage without the other part is HALF–TRUTH. (Again, read the entire verse.) Other sheep – must bring – Hear My voice – one fold – one Shepherd. (Key Phrase)

Symbolic of the Church – CHRIST's collected flock.

CHRIST then dealt with the Jews – "the lost sheep of the house of Israel," (Matthew 10, Matthew 15), but when the church has come in its fullness, it would include not only those sheep, but the "other sheep." The gospel was to be preached to all nations, JESUS knowing some would "hear" and come.

The picture of the church in Ephesians 2 and 3, Ezekiel 37:15–19, 22

Summary

For all who hear the call of CHRIST and cheerfully obey the summons—

There shall be one-fold – a single church, a single assembly of His disciples; ONE IN NAME: ONE IN THEIR CHARACTER, their life and their DESTINATION; with Jesus Christ as their good and only shepherd. The oneness taught here is the same as seen in other FIGURES of the Scripture.

There was but ONE ARK and all the saved were in the one ark. The reason for many folds today is that the people have heard the voices of men instead of CHRIST.

Hear CHRIST TODAY as He calls through the power of His cross and the preaching of His word.

FAMOUS LIES OF THE DEVIL

I. Introduction

    1. Three things about the devil

        a. Cunning, subtle Genesis 3:1

        b. No rest 1 Peter 5:8

        c. Deceiver – angel of light 2 Corinthians 11:14

    2. We must be careful lest we be deceived by Satan's lies.

    3. John 8:44

II. Discussion

    1.Everybody does it

        a. An effort to justify one's wrong

        b. Both at card parties, dance, etc.

        c. You don't see the best people of the church there, neither the worst of the world at church

        d. By attending worship Sunday or prayer meeting Wednesday night, these critics will see members they have never seen at dance parties, etc.

        e. There are many who live right.

        f. Can't establish right and truth on these grounds. Usually, the majority is wrong and anyway, two wrongs never make a right.

2. It doesn't make any difference what you believe, just so long as you are honest.

   a. It is a lie. Some men have their doctrine and GOD has his. Now who do you suppose will win?

   b. Truth would be no better than error as in Ephesians 4:14

   c. No false prophets

   d. Only the truth makes free John 8:32

   e. Must hear the truth Romans 10:17

III. Have a good time and then become a Christian

1. It implies that the life of sin is the happy and joyous life and the Christian life is dreary and sad

2. Pleasure for a season

3. Whatever crown sin may put on the heads of men, it will, at last, turn into a crown of thorns

4. No man can measure out to himself the amount of sin he will commit and compute the consequences, and then proceed according to plans.

5. When one opens his heart to let in just one sin, then like flies, a whole swarm comes in.

6. At first, no stronger than a spider web, later mesh of steel

7. Hard to get rid of a HABIT

8. This should be our prayer, "Keep back thy servant

also from presumptuous sins; let them not have dominion over me."

IV. Go ahead, you'll never know the difference a hundred years from now.

1. It is a lie – many could testify to this fact.

2. Sin never succeeds in the long run. Psalm37:7; 25, 36

3. The law of sowing and reaping must not be overlooked. Galatians 6:7–8

4. Thousands of sins may escape physical and social retribution, but they cannot escape the vengeance of GOD.

5. Fools make mockery of sin. When the ungodly shall be cast into the winepress of GOD's wrath, then shall they see the mockery of a successful sin.

6. Num. 32:23 "sin shall find you out."

V. Christianity is all right for little children, sick people and the weak

1. Used as insurance for protection

2. Greatest people were and are Christians – Father, Mother, Husband Wife, Citizen successful businessman.

3. Christianity is for all and the wise accept it. Will you push Satan with his lies into the background?

Conclusion.

1. Don't let Satan deceive you in any way.

2. Think of the importance of your soul. Matthew 10:28; Matthew 16:26

3. Fight against the devil Ephesians 6:10–17

PRESSING ON

Phil 3:12–14

Introduction

1. Christianity is a religion of progress.

Grow ... Go On ... Press Forward, etc.

2. To what should we press?

a. Service b. Full Growth c. Mark d. Victory

Discussion.

I. Must forget the past.

a. Mistakes

b. Good deeds.

c. Hurt from others.

II. By knowledge. Romans 10:1–3

Ignorance is always a hindrance. His. 4:6.

III. Lay aside every weight. Hebrews 12:1

Whatever weighs down our heart or affection to the earth

should be carefully avoided. Not necessarily a sin,

but something that hinders in our service to GOD.

TV. Sports, etc.

IV. Lay aside the sin. (The besetting sin).

One so easily to commit. Meets us on every turn.

  A. Lying. Something told or acted to deceive.

    1. Do you always fulfill your promises and threats?

    2. Were you really too sick to attend service?

    3. Were you really glad to see your company that came in unannounced?

    4. I've enjoyed having you; please do come again.

    5. I'd like to go, John, but it is impossible. People sometimes speak before thinking. Lie not one to another. Colossians 3:9

  B. Murmuring — always complaining.

    1. In the home, on the job, etc.

    2. Leaders not doing their duty.

    3. Preacher preaches too hard or too soft, too long or too short, doesn't dress to suit us.

  C. Tattling, busybodies carrying gossip.

    1. Keeps strife burning.

    2. Destroys homes, friendships and churches.

  D. Jawboning – TALK, TALK, TALK. Say and do not. Do you tell people or show them?

V. By patience. Endurance under trying circumstances. To a great extent, this will determine our eternal salvation.

VI. Leaving the first principles. Hey. 6:1

VII. Looking unto JESUS.

    1. He is our leader and example.

    2. He is our savior.

    3. Peter's experience in Matthew 14.

    4. He is the author and finisher of our faith.

Conclusion

    1. Don't press too far. 2 John 9.

        a. Must strive lawfully. @ Tim. 2:5.

    2. Must press unto the end. Matthew 24:13; Galatians 5:7; 6:9.

PRESSING ON – SERMON
Phil. 3:12–14

Introduction

1. In this passage, Paul reveals the secret of his great life and expresses the spirit of progress.

2. In achieving this success Paul had to forget somethings as related to the past and look to the future.

   a. From the beginning of time, GOD has wanted man to move forward, hence the arrangement of his lower limbs and the position of his eyes.

3. Christianity is a religion of progress.

   There is a goal ahead – Mark

   a. More CHRIST like in character and service.

   b. Full growth

   c. Crown of victory

   Things necessary in Pressing On.

Discussion

   I. Singleness of purpose. This one thing I do.

      1. There is power in concentration. The rays of the sun, if singly focused, would burn the world. Steam will move giant locomotives when

concentrated.

    a. GOD must be sought and served with all the heart. Hebrews 29:13; Matthew 22:37.

  2. A divided life is a weak life and is at the mercy of circumstances. James 1:8; Luke 8:14

II. Forgetting the Past. Paul forgot his race relations, religious connections, personal accomplishments, etc. because he could not use them in his Christian life. Philippians 3:4–10

  1. Past Accomplishments Paul – moral intellectual. Political, yet there was no vanity.

    a. Many boast of what has happened and fail to do any more good, stands if never spoken of again.

  2. Hurts and injuries from others. (Stripes, bruises, imprisonments, false charges, etc., no malice.)

    a. May be real or imaginary; intended or unintentional. Maybe someone made you angry – forgive and forget lest it harden into hate then murder.

  Ephesians 4:26, 27,29, 32. Ecclesiastes 7:9

  3. Our mistakes and failures (persecuted the church)

    a. Profit by them rather fold up.

    b. To fail in an endeavor does not mean that the goal is impossible. Men have failed many times in

their endeavors yet keep trying. DREAMS
SEED SERMONS

4. Our sins of yesterday.

a. If we turn to CHRIST by faith and repentance, He
will forgive and remember them no more.

III. Lay aside every weight and the sin.

1. That which hinders. Pleasure, duty, etc.

2. Sin of omission or commission

IV. Run with patience. (Possess the soul.)

V. Looking to JESUS. Leader, Example, Savior, Author
and Finisher of our faith. Peter's experience
Matthew 14

Conclusion

1. Must strive lawfully 2 Tim. 2:5

2. Must press unto the end. Matthew 24:13; Galatians
5:7; 6:9

3. You may have wasted many precious years in sin.
If you will only come to Him today, it makes no
difference how warped, bent, broken and blind you
may be at this moment; how stained and tarnished
and disfigured by the leprosy of sin; GOD can save.
THOUGH YOUR SINS BE AS SCARLET...

SOME THREES OF SIN

Introduction

Interesting to note the grouping of "threes" into which sin falls. This list may not be complete, but it suggests some things which we feel will be profitable to study.

Discussion

    I. Three Courses of Sin

        1. Sin – miss the mark

        2. Iniquity – a zigzag course or a departure from a straight line.

        3. Transgression – crossing a forbidden line or barrier, 1 John 3:4

    II. Three Avenues of Sin 1 John 2:16

        1. Lust of flesh

        2. Lust of the eye

        3. Pride of life

    III. The Actions of Sin Isaiah 1:1

        1. Sin of commission – overt acts

        2. Standing – neither walking nor sitting suggests the sin of indifference, Matthew 12:38

        3. Sitting – doing nothing, sin of omission Lack of conformity to the will of GOD James 4:17

IV. Three Persons Affective

How can I do this great wickedness and sin against GOD?

1. GOD, Genesis 39:9; Psalm 51:4

2. Neighbor, Romans 13:10 love works no ill to neighbor

3. Self, Ezekiel 18:20

Conclusion

Three things to be done about sin

1. Repent of – turn from, have them washed away Acts 17:30; 3:19; 22:16

2. Confess them 1 John 1:9

3. Confess as public as sin is

CORRECTING MISTAKES

Introduction

1. As long as we are humans, we are subject to mistakes. We never get too great. To never admit to a wrong is to pose as one divine. To admit that we are wrong proves that we are wiser today than we were yesterday.

2. When a person learns that he has made a mistake, he should take immediate steps to correct it.

3. "Correct your mistakes before you leave this building."

4. Naaman was a great man; captain of the host, great with his master, honorable, mighty with valor. We also learn that he was a leper. Leprosy was a dreaded disease that knew no human cure. (In many respects a type of sin.)

5. In the process of being cured, he made many mistakes. Among his victories, he had brought captive out of Israel a little maid who now waited on his wife. She spoke to her mistress about a prophet in Israel. (2 Kings 5:1-14) You know the story. When he sought help from the prophet, he did not do as the prophet told him to do.

I. He went to the wrong place.

1. He went to the king of Israel. Verses 5–7

2. To further testify to his greatness, he carried ten talents of silver, 6,000 pieces of gold, and ten changes of raiment.

3. Through the years people have gone to the wrong place: mourner's bench, altar, in the valley all alone – men of the world and their knowledge.

4. CHRIST is the way and the door to heaven.

5. We must learn of Him through the book. John 5:39; Isaiah 34:16; Hebrews 10:7

Finally reached the right place and told what to do.

II. Misunderstood the Remedy.

1. "I thought" v. 11 "I had this all figured out."

2. He was wroth because it was not according to his thoughts.

People set aside the law of GOD for their thoughts.
Church, Name, Baptism, Music

III. He wanted to substitute.

1. Dipping in Jordan for a miracle.

2. Manual for the Bible. Man against GOD. Acts 5:29

3. Burial in water with S. & P.

4. A thing substituted is vain.

5. Don't add. Rev, 22:18–19

(Older denominations, a book other than the Bible)
GOD has always sounded the warning of
changing His will.

IV. Wanted to dictate his place of cure.

1. Abana and Pharpar v. 12

2. There is no choice.

3. CHRIST said My church, Ephesians 5:23. "I like
this one – larger, famous choir, eloquent
preacher, etc."

V. Thought the plan was too simple. v. 13, 1 Corinthians
1:21–29–31; 2:5

1. Many people today think the plan of salvation is
too simple. "Thou art the CHRIST." H.B.R.C.B

BE BAPTIZED – Turn and come all the way back. Then
start again in the right direction.

THE IMPORTANCE OF GOD'S WORD

Introduction

   1. Man is warned against letting the LORD's word slip.

      a. Drift away from them

      b. Leak out!

   2. In every situation of life, at all times, and in all places, we should not suffer the word to slip.

   3. The danger of letting it slip may arise from many sources

13th Chapter of Matthew

   1. Lack of understanding Matthew 13:19 Satan takes away.

   2. The care of the world and, oxen, wives Luke 14:16–20

   3. Tribulation or persecution Matthew 13:20–21

   4. Prejudice Matthew 13:11–Matthew 12:13

   5. Compromise or a desire to please men

I. Two great truths mentioned in v. 2

   1. Word was "Steadfast" definite, settled, not wavering

    2. Every transgression and disobedience…reward

       a. Commission 1 John 3:4

       b. Omission John 4:17; 2 Peter 2:4–6

II. Salvation is great but will not save unless man is disposed to listen.

    1. Book must be read to be helpful

    2. Sun drives out darkness, but we must open our eyes.

    3. Vegetables will sustain life, but not in the garden, must be eaten and digested

    4. Medicine in the bottle will not cure.

III. The Question Carries Its Own Answer (no worry)

    1. Same as thief, murderer, atheist, scoffer (sick man)

    2. Neglect has the power to ruin and destroy – teeth, health, friendship, farms, homes.

Conclusion

    1. Neglect will condemn many in the judgment

       a. Matthew 7:24–27 heard but neglected

       b. Matthew 25:41–46 "fed Me not"

    2. Christian commanded to work Philippians 2:12

    3. Don't neglect today.

PEOPLE CHRIST PRAISED

Luke 7

John 12:42–50

Praise is a wonderful thing, especially if it is coming from the right person (one who is sincere and truthful, expecting nothing in return). Praise at the right time can be like spring rain on dry soil.

1. Mark Twain once said that he could live for a week on a good solid compliment.

2. A man was said to have a special drawer in his desk for "<u>rainy day letters</u>" letters in which his friends had praised him, thanked him, or encouraged him. These he would pull out at this low points and reread.

3. Phyllis McGively said, "They can turn a bleak morning into June or nourish the spirit and body like vitamins."

It's dangerous to live for praises, an indication that we are seeking society's approval. Psychiatrists and counselors see a steady stream of emotionally sick people who are trying to please everybody.

A certain amount of sensitivity to public opinion is

normal. But caution should be exercised lest we find ourselves loving the "praise of men more than the praise of GOD." John 12:42–43 A distinguishing characteristic of the Pharisees of JESUS' day was fear of the people. Pilate.

This spirit invades the church! Many turn away from desiring the approval of GOD toward wanting the approval of men. This has brought about a weakening of spiritual strength. While we are thinking about what men might be thinking about us, we forget to ask what GOD might be thinking about us. THIS equals reputation verse character!

We know GOD loves us, yes, still few of us have thrust our lives into the bright healing light of His love. We scurry around in the shadows living cramped, cribbed, unhappy Christian lives – because we believe it is easier to build a reputation before men than to have a character which is approved of GOD. It takes courage to ask with complete honesty, "Just what does GOD think of me?"

Luke pulled together in one chapter (7) three people for whom JESUS had words of praise. A study of these three characters and asking why they were praised may give us a clue to GOD's opinion of men.

1. An army officer verse 2–9 had many good qualities – JESUS said, "He is worthy." From Matthew we learn that:

   a. As a Roman, he had crossed a racial line and built a

synagogue for the Jews.

b. Loved his servants because he sought help for one who was sick.

c. Didn't feel worthy to approach JESUS.

d. Note his unquestionable faith – "Speak the word."

Jesus praises his faith. Faith is an authority greater than any military authority – faith in the word of JESUS, believing His word carried power to heal, even at a distance. Maybe even with all these good traits, JESUS compliments the man because he brought his problems to Him. (Character vs Faith)

2. The preacher, John the Baptist (verse 17–28)

a. Prepared for the coming of CHRIST by his preaching – calling men to repentance.

CHRIST met with opposition but think what it would have been like if John had not prepared a people.

b. He was in prison and lived in hard physical conditions (Matthew 11:2–6) because he had told a wicked king the truth – he was no one's <u>kept court priest</u>. He had courage conviction and humility, the Levites of Judges 17:7; 18:18–20. (Courage verse confidence)

3. The woman of Luke 7:36–50, there isn't much to praise, "SINNER."

Knowing JESUS was present, came in with alabaster

box, etc. (Putting on a show, out of her place)

etc. [Simon & friends]

JESUS looked beyond the sins, the emotional

outburst and saw something beautiful.

a. Love – rather than being out of her mind v. 47 –

Love before forgiveness and love after

forgiveness (Parable of JESUS in answer to

Simon's concern).

But again, the praise is given because she brought her sins to Him. CHRIST complimented us by dying for us. (Romans 5:7–8) He waits for us to open our minds, hearts, loves, every corner of our being to His forgiving love.

Oh, how we should desire the traits of these three, however, realizing all lies in an acceptance of GOD. He accepts us even before we achieve a spotless character – we must accept GOD's acceptance of us with our unworthiness (problems), our doubts and sins. They did. Luke 5:1–6; 1 John 1:6–10.

Let us make the tangible act of accepting his love.

PRODIGAL SON

Angry, Childish, Jealous – Elder Son

Couldn't be happy that his brother had come home (your son).

True in some families today – one who has always been there for their parents – gets upset when they shower affection on one/those who drop in once or twice a year, sis. Trice's confession and the paper article – Lady Who Was Always on Hand to Look to the Needs of Her Elderly parents – Cook and carry them food while others came by at their convenience and brought nothing and would sometimes eat what was found there (even meal on wheels meals).

CHURCH – we who are in comparison, more innocent than others, seldom know how to show compassion toward those who have been overt sinners and then repent. (I can't worship with them…; they shouldn't be allowed to be active in anything.) Though we aren't guilty of what we consider "big" sins, can we say we are sinlessly perfect? (Sins of thought, words, and attitude). We that are without sin, let us cast the first stone. Out of anger and ill feeling, he said a lot of things that might be questioned.

1. How "your son" (not my brother) had wasted the money with harlots

2. "I" never transgressed thee… if this statement were true then the elder brother's spirit "now" should have been the same as his father's.

Sometimes, we can't see the forest for the trees.

Note: For further treatise of this parable, see "The Culmination of the Treatise on Grace" in the Table of Contents.

REACHING FOR THE SON IN '81
Phil. 3:13–16

This sermon was delivered by Bro. Graham Q. McGill in 1981 so the title was appropriate for that audience at that time. However, the goal of every Christian should be to become more like CHRIST every year, so a fitting title for this same sermon if delivered the first Sunday of this year could have been "Striving to Do More in '24." If we haven't made very much progress in this direction, observe that time is rapidly getting away.

There are possibilities around us yet unexploded, (not even explored). The term explode is used in reference to <u>bringing something into being, something that is possible, but has not yet been accomplished</u>.

1. Becoming a strong spiritual Christian. Convince yourself that you want to be a better Christian. No aim – no progress. Aim at nothing and accomplish it with amazing accuracy.

   a. Fill your mind with worthwhile things. 1Peter 2:1– 3 – Isaiah 1:1–2; Jude 20–21; 2 Peter 1:5–9 Realize your inadequacies and aim.

   b. Pray – not Xerox prayers James 5:16–18

c. Believe in GOD Mark 9:23–24

d. Helping others

2. Church Attendance

3. Church Growth (don't want swelling). Not up to me to make it grow, but up to us.

Let me again challenge you to pick out one person, good or bad' and try to reach them for CHRIST. Invite them to come; share with them what you believe – don't skin them alive, arrange a class to be taught by you or preacher or leading brother, whatever. Try!

In our present state, individual or congregation wise, if JESUS were to make a visit to us today, what would He find most consistent with His goals or will for us?

To reach the SON, at least three things are necessary:

1. Do you want to know what the Bible says?

2. Will you believe?

3. Will you do it?

This will work with a lot of things.

Do you know and believe what it says about:

GOD's gift of love; the church that grew out of that love; GOD's plan for saving man and granting him entrance into the church; the Christian's life and work?

SAVED BY FEAR

Hebrews 11:7

Noah Moved by Fear (fear and trembling)

Introduction

1. A few years ago, there appeared an article in Life entitled, "A Chair that Scares Them."

   a. Story of a kind of shock therapy for hard core delinquents

   b. They were taken on a tour of the Colorado State Prison. They were shown the death house and were invited to sit in the "death chair." This reached some boy that everything else had failed to.

2. What effects would it have on the life of mankind if they could be taken on a tour of Hell?

3. Let's take a word picture tour of hell. The Bible tells us much about the nature of hell and how terrible it will really be to spend eternity there. Hell is real; no hell – no lost.

Discussion

I. The Trial of Sentencing

1. Brought before the throne Matthew 25:31–46;

Revelation 20:11–15

a. The evidence of our unworthiness is presented.

b. The number of times we refused the opportunity to be justified (not yet)

c. Number of times you have forsaken the assembly, refused to give, mistreated someone.

2. Hear the verdict, "Depart from Me!!"

II. How long is our term?

1. Same words used to describe the duration of Heaven is used for hell.

a. Matthew 25:26; Thessalonians 1:9 Everlasting destruction

b. Revelation 20:10

c. Mark 9:43

III. Nature of Hell

1. Outer darkness

2. Weeping and gnashing

3. Something beyond comprehension

STOP, LOOK, AND LISTEN
Jeremiah 6:16

Introduction

A sign that has been seen in many places, designed to arrest or attract one's attention suggests a matter of great importance – the results of which can/will be beneficial to those who heed it.

Many have lost their lives because they did not heed the sign at a railroad crossing. Some may have missed out on some good bargains along the way. Our society is traveling at a very fast pace so that we miss out on the everyday beauties of life. Need to take the time to smell the roses; hear the singing of the birds, etc.

In all these things we can see GOD, our Creator and keeper. Scripture teaches us that GOD takes care of the flowers and has concern for the sparrows.

Taking a closer look at the lesson, let's look at each word in the title and see what lessons may be gained.

STOP

To stop means to cease activity or operation; come to an end; discontinue.

Cease evil and ungodliness (1 Peter 10–11, 12)

Righteousness is good for its leaders to longevity of life (love life and see good days).

Refrain his tongue from evil and lips that they speak no guile.

The evils of the tongue profane speech – speech that reflects upon the glory and the name of GOD. Gross and wicked speech (filthy/foul mouth). Ex.20:7; Matthew 5:34; uncharitable speech designed to defame and disgrace others – Ephesians 4:31; James 4:11; 1 Peter 2:1 And these are of two sorts – open railings and slander and secret, fruitless talk. Ephesians 4:29, Lips and Guile (deceit, lying). Don't bear false witness, Exodus 20:17; 23:1; Proverbs 24:28. Lying, Isaiah 101:7; Colossians 3:9; Ephesians 4:25.

James said if a man can control his tongue, he can control the whole body. Stop while time lingers, and mercy pleads. Romans 13:11 Time to awake out of sleep – CHRIST said, "Behold, I come quickly." Revelation 22:7, 10–12

LOOK

To look means to behold, examine, inspect view. Matthew 6:19; Colossians 3:1

1. Look at eternal values 2 Corinthians 4:17

We are often unhappy because our vision is wrongly focused (center vision and marginal vision).

2. Look for Truth – By it we are made free. John 8:31–

32 (Truth is in the word.) John 17:17; 1 Peter
1:21,23,25 Truth about the church, the name, plan of
Salvation, and what is required of Christians to be
saved.

3. Look for opportunity to do good. Galatians 6:10 Many
opportunities pass us by. Sickness, death,
community projects

4. Look to JESUS: 1. As our only Savior and our
encouragement as we run the Christian race. John
3:14–16; Hebrews 12:2

LISTEN

To listen means to give ear to; attend closely for the
purpose of hearing; make a conscious effort or endeavor to
hear, (can hear and not hear). How often have you heard and
yet, didn't hear, (not paying attention.) "He that hath an ear
to hear, let him hear." Matthew 11:15

1. Listen to the Word of GOD. "Incline your ears."
Psalm 78:1 He that hath an ear, let him hear. (Plea
to those of the seven churches) Isaiah 1:1.2;
Proverbs 2:1–2

2. Listen to wise counsel and encouragement to live for
JESUS.

3. Also counsel about the choices of life (associates,
drugs, sex, courtship, marriage, etc.)

4. Listen as <u>CHRIST Calls for YOU</u>! Matthew 11:28–
   30; Revelation 22:17

Listen as He knocks at the door of your heart! Final
appeal made from Hebrews 6:16

Stand ye

See

Ask

Walk

TEACHING AND ADMONISHING ONE ANOTHER
Colossians 3:16

Introduction

This is one of Paul's prison epistles written to instruct and encourage the churches he had knowledge of. I suppose the subject of this text is "teaching and admonishing one another." (Paul and Silas) Teaching and admonishing is modified by the phrase, "Let the word of CHRIST dwell in you richly in all wisdom."

This enables one to teach. Without CHRIST's word dwelling richly in a person, he cannot properly teach another.

Let's see the comparison between Ephesians 5:18–19 and Colossians 16.

Spirit and Word – They work together! However, speaking to one's self is not enough; he must teach and admonish others.

Teaching is important – no other way to gain the religion of CHRIST. (Commission, commit to faithful men, etc. in teaching, instructing, and helping is involved.)

Not only in presenting the Scripture are people taught, but also in singing. Text in Psalms, Hymns and Spiritual Songs.

It may not be proper to separate the three, but many have

made the attempt.

Psalm – Sentiment not without rhyme (as O.T. psalm)

Hymns – Giving praise to the LORD, for example, How Great THOU Art.

Spiritual Songs Song that presents any spiritual truth.

Singing – No mention of Mechanical Instruments (I've noticed in recent years that churches have given more attention to their singing workshops, etc.)

WHAT WAIT I FOR?

Psalm39:7

Wait may be defined in several ways – (time spent in anticipation of) in a sense of delaying or lingering.

1. Waiting is often necessary – preparing for duty (even in the LORD's church), harvest (crops and souls), becoming of age.

2. Otherwise, waiting can be disastrous – medical attention, escaping a burning house, putting an automobile in proper mechanical condition and OBEDIENCE to the gospel to the saving of the soul.

3. The Psalmist of the text speaks of the brevity of life and the importance/urgency of obedience.

4. Salvation is as simple as coming to Jesus Christ on His terms – the JESUS Who died to save us from sin and death.

This may sound somewhat personal, but those of you who are in a lost condition, ask yourself, "What Wait I For?"

Discussion

I. I See Too Many Hypocrites

The first thought is to say, "There is always room for one more" BUT...

1. Hypocrites are something that goes with the territory! There were Ananias and Sapphira. Acts 5:1–11 Hypocrisy may even be seen in the home.

   a. Each person must stand the test for himself.

II. Waiting Until I Get Good Enough

1. You've got a long wait! How long have you been trying, 20, 30 or 40 years? It hasn't worked and never will! We need a Force greater than ourselves.

III. I Have Too Much to Give Up!

1. Anything you need to give up, you ought to give up. All GOD wants you to give up is that which is bad for you – poison to you, etc. "What shall a man give in exchange for his soul?"

IV. Waiting Until I Learn More

1. How much do you need to know? If you know you are a sinner, CHRIST made salvation possible; this salvation can be acquired by F.R.B. (faith, repentance, baptism) and you are then added to the church, you know enough. Sometimes you must learn after initial obedience. Colossians 1:9; 2:6; 2 Pet.3:18

V. Waiting for a More Convenient Season/Time

   1. So did Felix as recorded in Acts 24

   2. When/what is a more convenient time? How do you know it will come? (Didn't for Felix.)

GOD says "NOW," and Satan says "Later."

VI. Waiting to Feel Right

   1. The feeling should begin with poverty of spirit, mourning – godly sorrows. Feel good because we've obeyed GOD and have His approval!

Conclusion

Through the years, many have waited: Some had the opportunity to make the change – others waited too late. (Jim Collins)

What about you? Story of young man who had his life planned, but without GOD. Finish college, practice my profession, become wealthy and share with family, retire, and write some books, spend time with grandchildren ... DIE. He planned as if he was the architect of time ...

The waiting Savior says, "Come."

WHEN GOD LAUGHS AT MAN

Introduction

The Scriptures depict GOD as a laughing GOD. Isaiah 2:1–4; Psalm 37:12–13; Proverbs 1:24–26

In Psalm 37:13, the Hebrew word for laugh, *śāḥaq,* pronounced "saw–hkak," is defined as deride, mock, make sport. GOD's laugh is one of condemnation. There is a difference between the laugh of GOD and the laugh of men. Men laugh at the trivial, but GOD at things which are most serious.

There is also a difference between GOD's laugh and GOD's smile. I don't think the Bible ever speaks of GOD smiling, yet we think of His smile when He approves of any good thing man has to do and does it well. Abel and his offering; Abraham and offering of his son; John the Baptist and the fulfillment of his mission; the apostles and their work, especially Paul and his dedication; dedicated families who rear their children to love and respect the Church; gospel ministers who give themselves for the cause; etc.

But it is a sad thing for man when GOD laughs – it is condemnation for our sins. May it never fall on us. The very thought of a laughing GOD is enough to make the blood run cold and strike terror in the hearts of men.

Discussion

The laugh of GOD is not one-sided!

1. GOD does not laugh at man until man laughs at GOD.

   a. Rulers of the world, Isaiah 2:2; great empires have fallen because men have lived as though there were no GOD. Herod, Acts 12. (America could be next.)

2. The Christian who fails to obey the commands of GOD laughs at Him.

   a. Christians are exhorted to be faithful unto death. (Revelation 2:10) Some such people, when talked to admit they are hell bound, but do nothing about it. – They are laughing at GOD. GOD uses the threat of hell as an incentive to do right. But man seems undisturbed at this threat. (You're kidding – you won't do that when hell becomes a reality; then GOD will be laughing.)

   b. GOD demands that His people give liberally as they purpose. But how many people are concerned about the contribution of the Church being up or down? Many care not. Whether the budget is reached or not and thus, use their money for themselves. The amount of Scripture devoted to the subject shows its importance. Yet man laughs at GOD. Things begin to close in on you, hard to make ends meet; foreclosure on and reclaiming of property.

c. Preaching Gospel to the Lost!

When we exclude this from our church program and budget, we merely laugh at GOD.

d. GOD demands that His people put His kingdom first and attend the services of the Church. Usually, the preacher who emphasizes this is called a hobby rider. But if we consider this lightly, we laugh at GOD.

3. The sinner who rejects the pardon of the gospel laughs at GOD. He sent His Son to provide salvation from sin for every man. Now He commands, counsels, and begs man to turn to Him. Man closes his mind to this and thousands of a given LORD's day morning throughout the world will turn their backs to the invitation.

What will you do?

GOD forbid that the words of Proverbs 11:24 fall upon any of you here as we all must face GOD in judgment.

WHOSE SERVANT ARE YOU?

Romans 6:16

Based upon the text, the question is raised and in the same text, Paul answers the question once and for all. WE ARE THE SERVANTS of the one we obey.

There is no neutral ground. We are servants of GOD, or we are servants of the Devil. Matthew 12:30.

It became necessary in Moses' day to call upon the people to show where they stood. Ezekiel. 32:26

This is a question that needs to be thought on seriously. It seems that so few of us are <u>thinking</u>. We are taking the way of least resistance – the way that gives us the satisfaction NOW, and we aren't looking at the consequences at the end of the road. Let's note Proverbs 1:29–31. (Take the time to read these words prayerfully and thoughtfully.) Galatians 6:7–8

Let me present a parable at this point – on one side there is a dear sweet mother – the one that went through the valley of the shadow of death to give me life – one who would starve to death to keep me from being hungry – one who gave up sleep that I might be made comfortable on occasions. A Mother like this is the most excellent of them all, though many have done well, (whether she is yours or mine.)

Now, over against this mother I present another character – one who tried to destroy my life as soon as I was born – and all along life's way, he has sought to put germs of all kind in the water I drink and food I eat hoping to bring death and end to my earthly career – he has slandered me to my back; has tried to destroy my good name – he has thought only evil toward me and not one time has he sought to do me good.

What would you think if I forgot my mother because of my admiration and devotion to my enemy who is daily on my heart and in my life, while Mother is forgotten because I have no time for her? Mother has lain wake at night while I was out doing the wishes of the enemy.

Such a story is unthinkable, and you probably thought it foolish as I tried to tell it BUT THINK!

GOD ought to be served because He gave us life making us in His likeness; He sustains the life He gave us – it is His food we eat, His water, His air, His sunshine…etc. Acts 17:28. He gave us salvation through the giving of His son; He keeps us saved as JESUS intercedes daily for us.

What has the Devil done for us? Can you think of one reason why we should serve him? Yet, many are serving him. Those forsaking the assembly for pleasurable involvement – those forgetting to keep book with GOD and give the first fruit of their increase – those spending the LORD's money on their lusts and pleasures – those who hate their brothers – those who don't have the courage to make a full surrender of their lives to GOD – those who have no love for lost souls.

THINK and come to yourself as the prodigal son did, realize your condition, and act. Don't know if the son came to himself because he realized he was in a hog pen or that he realized that he was in a hog pen only after he came to himself.

But the question still rings, "Whose servant are you?" You are the servant of the one Whose wishes are being accomplished in you! It's either GOD or the Devil.

Decide now! It will be too late when you get to the judgment. Matthew 7:22, 23; 25:1–12.

Wages of sin is death – Gift of GOD is eternal life…

It's a matter of obedience or disobedience!

Now is the time. Felix, Acts 26 and Agrippa, Acts 24.

Some Women Needed,
Some Not, in the Church

Introduction

1. A great deal of praise is due the women of today for the part they are playing in the affairs of the church. The church is composed largely of women.
2. However, all women aren't a credit to the church, therefore, the subject.
3. The Bible is filled with the lives of many women, good and bad.

Discussion

I. The Negative Side

   A. Women who are instigators of wickedness like Jezebel of the Old Testament. 1 Kings 21

   Women are behind many wicked schemes in the church when others are fronting for them.

   B. Women who discourage their husbands like Job's wife. Job 2:9

   It can easily be done.

   They don't appreciate your work.

   They don't accept your suggestions.

   They don't let you do certain things.

C. Deceitful women like Delilah who make use of any underhanded practice intended to mislead.

D. Quarrelsome women like Euodia and Syntyche who persecute the preacher for preaching the truth Philippians 4

E. Cruel women like Herodias who persecute the preacher for preaching the truth Matthew 14:1–12

II. The Positive Side

A. Women who teach their children Scripture like Eunice and Lois 2 Tim. 1:15; 3:15
Training starts in the home.

B. Those who place hearing the word of the LORD above cooking and housework like Mary.

C. Women who show hospitality to GOD's servants like the Shunamite woman 2 Kings 4

D. Personal workers like Priscilla Acts 18

E. Those who respect their husbands and are subject unto them like Sarah. 1 Peter 3:6

F. Modest women like Vashti Esther 1

MAY THE WORK I'VE DONE SPEAK FOR ME

Thank You

for Reading!

www.TMPbooks.com

If you enjoyed this book,

please leave a brief review.

Made in the USA
Columbia, SC
15 June 2024

36660148R10089